Introduction to
Dressmaking

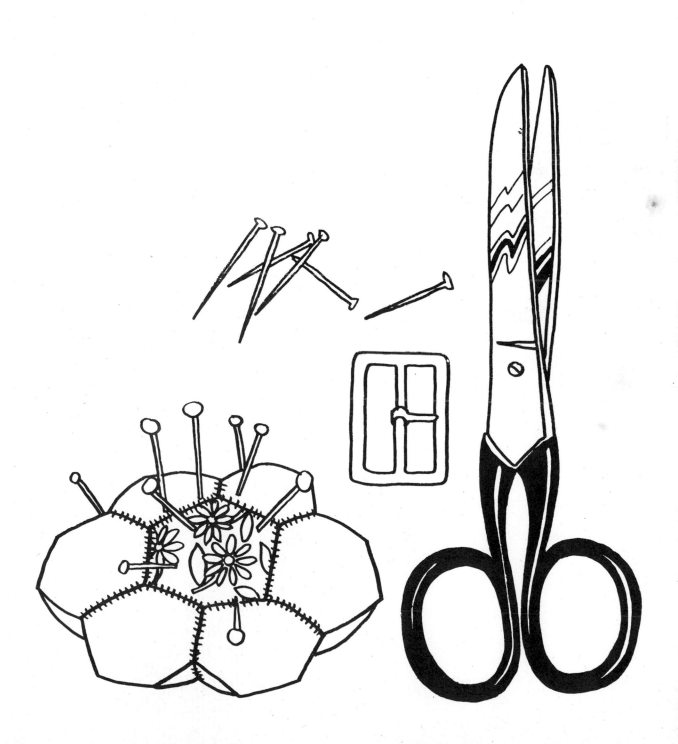

Introduction to
Dressmaking

Golden Hands Books

Marshall Cavendish
London and New York

Contributors

Text: Marilyn Berry; Ida Coyston; Jane Kirkwood

Illustrations: Elizabeth Embleton; Terry Evans; Barbara Firth; Anna Kostal; Eileen Poston; Pauline Rosenthal

Photographs: John Carter; Roger Charity; Richard Domer; Frances Ross Duncan; Richard Dunckley; Tony Horth; Chris Lewis; Peter Rand.

Edited by Susan Simmons

Published by Marshall Cavendish Publications Limited, 58 Old Compton Street, London W1V 5PA

Some of this material has previously appeared in the publications Golden Hands Monthly and Golden Hands New Guide.

First printing 1975

ISBM 0 85685 128 0

Printed in Great Britain by The Artisan Press Ltd.

Introduction

How often in dressmaking does the finished garment just not live up to your expectations—perhaps the collar does not sit right, the hem not hang correctly or the dress as a whole not fit as perfectly as you'd hoped.

Whether you're a beginner or an expert, this book sets out to answer your questions and to help you achieve the best possible results from home dressmaking. From choosing your equipment and handling fabrics to the final press, each stage of dressmaking is dealt with in detail: patterns and how to adapt them to ensure a really perfect fit; cutting out; when and how to use linings and interlinings; inserting zips and how to ensure the best finishes with collars, cuffs and sleeves.

Decorative finishes are also included. From working with those difficult fabrics such as velvet and lace to making rouleau buttons and button loops as an unusual finish to a coat or dress, how to ensure a belt is placed on the garment to flatter each individual figure and how to add piping to brighten up a dress or skirt plus lots of ideas on how to save money and add an original touch to your clothes.

And, for the truly adventurous, there's a section on tailoring. Covered step-by-step and fully illustrated, it ensures that each garment can be completed successfully with the minimum of inconvenience and expense.

Contents

Dressmaking

Tailoring

Essential equipment

It is important to choose even the most basic sewing equipment with care. Tools of a high quality will ensure a more professional finish and will make the job easier and more pleasant. The tools will also last longer if they are well-made.

There are many sewing aids available which are useful to have if you can afford them, but the basic requirements are as follows.

Scissors

Three pairs are necessary and they must be sharp.

A small pair for snipping threads, trimming seam allowances and cutting buttonholes (although there are special buttonhole scissors which can be adjusted to cut any size buttonhole).

A medium pair with 10 to 15cm (4 to 5in) blades for general, all purpose work.

A large pair of shears with 18cm (7in) blades for cutting out pattern pieces.

Never use dressmaking scissors for any other purpose as this will blunt the blades.

Tape measure

Choose a fibre glass tape measure with brass ends as this will not stretch as most other types do. Also, choose one that gives metric as well as imperial measurements.

Thimble

Choose a silver or steel one for preference. The correct position is when the needle is pressed into the fabric by the side of the thimble.

Pins

Use sharp, fine steel dressmaker's pins and not those sold in stationers. Pins are usually 2cm ($\frac{3}{4}$in) long but lillikens 1.3cm ($\frac{1}{2}$in) long can be used for light-weight fabrics. Pins with coloured bead heads are useful for lacy fabrics where ordinary ones can slip through and often lie unseen.

Needles

There are needles for every type of sewing so be sure to choose the right one for perfect results. Sewing faults can often be attributed to a blunt or too thick needle.

For general hand sewing use Sharps and keep the whole range of sizes in the sewing box.

For fine work use a Between No.9. These little needles pick up tiny threads easily and they have small eyes which take very fine thread.

'Straws' or 'milliners', used in hat-making, are long and fine with a small eye designed for sewing though buckram and thick layers of fabric. They are also used for tacking, especially in tailoring.

For sewing stretch fabrics use either a very fine needle when sewing by hand or a ball-point needle in the machine. This avoids the puckering and stitch missing often experienced when using an ordinary machine needle where the sharp point catches the threads of the fabric.

Suede and leather need a strong needle with a really sharp point, preferably a 'glovers' needle that is three-sided.

It is more economical to purchase needles in one size packets rather than in packets of graded sizes. Make sure that the needles are always in good condition by keeping them in a warm, dry place in a felt-or flannel-paged needlebook to protect them from rusting or becoming blunt.

Tailor's chalk

This is used for marking pattern instructions such as notches, alterations and hems.

Sewing thread

Deciding on the correct thread to use for a particular piece of work involves more than matching the colour to the fabric. There are several different types of thread on the market, each one for a specific function. No.40 mercerised cotton is the most widely used and is available in over 350 fast colours. Most versatile, it can be used for all natural fibre, medium-weight fabrics such as cotton, wool, flannel, gaberdine, twills, denim, tweeds and cord. With this thread, vary the needle size, de-pending on the fabric, from a No.8 hand-sewing needle (11 to 14 machine) for medium-weights to a No.6 or 7 hand needle (16 machine) for heavier fabrics and a No.4 or 5 hand needle (No.18 machine) for really heavy fabrics.

For more delicate fabrics such as net, organdie, lace, lawn and chiffon, it is essential to use No.50 mercerised thread or pure silk with a No.10 hand (No.11 machine) needle. Other lighter weight fabrics such as cotton gingham, muslin, crepe and fine wool need this thread but with a No.9 hand needle (No.11 to 14 machine).

Synthetic fabrics are best sewn with synthetic threads. Use No.60 for very fine fabrics and No.40 for everything else.

Pure silk should never be sewn with anything but pure silk thread which should also be used for fine wool. Ideally, silk is the best sewing thread for all sewing jobs as it is exceptionally strong but at the same time soft, so it does not harm the fibres of the fabric.

Buttonhole twist is used for working hand-sewn buttonholes on medium to heavy fabrics or for sewing on buttons. Machine embroidery cotton is used not only for embroidery but for working machine buttonholes. A wide variety of other threads such as Lurex, knitting wool, buttonhole twist and hand embroidery threads can be wound onto the machine spool for top stitching or decorative embroidery on garments.

Tacking cotton in white and colours is a must; not only is it cheaper than mercerised thread but it is weaker and therefore simple to break and remove after the stitching is done. Do not use red tacking cotton on light coloured fabrics as it will stain.

Sewing machine

The sewing machine is the most expensive item of equipment needed for home sewing and dressmaking and considerable thought should be given to the requirements before the final purchase is made. Choose the most useful machine for your own particular needs. If you are only going to use the machine for making the occasional pair of

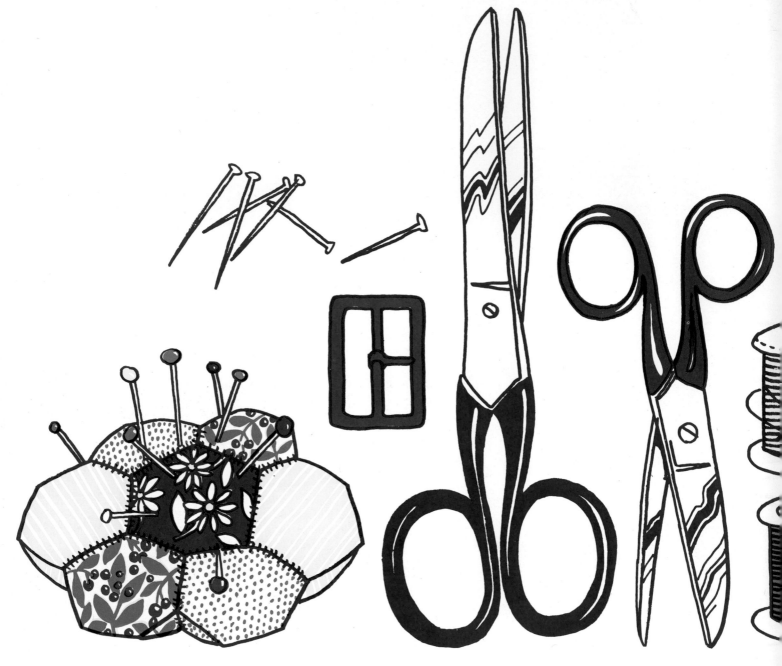

curtains or cushion cover, it is a waste of money to purchase an expensive automatic machine whereas, if you intend to use the machine for multi-purposes and to experiment with machine embroidery, it is worth considering a fully automatic. The wider the variety of stitches and quantity of stitches and gadgets, the more expensive the machine so, if they are not going to be used, do not pay for them but look for a machine that does just what you want it to do for you.

The four most important features of any machine are:-

Type—Flat-bed or free-arm.
Category—For plain sewing or for more complex usage.
Portability—To carry about or merely move.

Function—For light or heavy sewing or for free embroidery.

Type
Flat-bed machines are traditional in style and are cheaper than free-arm models.
Free-arm are new in style. They have a small arm rather like a sleeve board that is raised above the base of the machine. This comes in useful for attaching sleeves to armholes and for sewing small children's clothes. The arm can be surrounded by a clip-on plate which makes a larger working surface.

Category
Straight stitch. Machines will only sew a straight stitch.

Zig-zag. Buttonholes can be made but not automatically; the work has to be turned. Embroidery patterns can be made manually by moving the zig-zag lever while sewing but it is difficult. Most machines have a three position zig-zag stitch, which means that the needle can be positioned in the centre to the left or to the right. These three settings can also be used when working straight stitch.
Semi-automatic, minimatic or utility stitch. Machines have about one to five embroidery and/or utility stitches. The embroidery stitches make decorative patterns and the utility stitches are for functional purposes. Both stitches are formed automatically by discs or cams which are generally built into these machines.

Popular utility stitches are:

Stretch or triple stitch—Used for seaming stretch fabrics where great elasticity is required.

Elastic stitch—Used for sewing on elastic and for mending.

Blind hemming—For invisibly stitched hemlines.

Over-edge stitch—For simultaneously joining and finishing the edges of fabrics. Automatic buttonholes can be made on some of these machines. By pre-setting control knobs, the needle automatically zig-zags to the left and to the right, moves forwards and backwards and bar tacks the ends, without the fabric being turned. Many of these machines take double needles, which give twin lines of stitching and also pin tucks.

Some utility stitch machines can also make a chain stitch by dispensing with the bobbin. Being a single thread stitch, it is easy to unpick and can therefore be used for tacking.

Fully automatic. These machines are the most expensive to buy. They have about 10 to 20 embroidery and utility stitches and can make an automatic buttonhole. The discs or cams, which are automatically set to make the embroidery and utility stitches, can be permanently built into the machine or may be loose and have to be inserted.

Pressing aids

A strong, sturdy ironing board that can be adjusted to a number of heights suitable for individual comfort, whether for sitting or standing, is essential.

A sleeve board is necessary too, as well as a pressing mitt or ham (for pressing curved seams) and a seam roll (for pressing seams open to avoid the edges of the seam allowance showing through to the right side of the garment). A pressing block is required for banging steam back into the material when working with thick fabrics, but the back of a heavy, wooden clothes brush will work just as well. The heavier the iron, the better and it should be a dry not a steam one. A quantity of cotton pressing cloths (well-washed so that there is no dressing left in them) are essential and a fine wool pressing cloth is useful to prevent shine on woollen fabrics.

Choosing and handling fabrics

Most fabrics are too expensive to take risks with but care in preparation and making sure of the correct stitch tension, needle size and thread for the particular fabric will lessen the problems. The choice of fabric, suiting it to the design and knowing how to handle it are the most important initial steps in dressmaking. However well the garment is sewn together, if the fabric is wrong for the style, or for a particular figure, the result will be disastrous.

Suiting fabric to style and figure
Take a critical look at your figure before purchasing fabric and do not choose a mini-print if built on Junoesque lines. Similarly, a petite figure will tend to look swamped and top heavy if dressed in a boldly patterned design. Drape a length of the fabric over you to see if the colour and the pattern suit you and, at the same time, bear in mind the actual garment to be made. For instance do not choose a light-weight jersey fabric for a casual jacket which will get a lot of wear and tear.
Considerable thought should also be given to choosing a style—a soft, flowing, simply styled dress can carry a bold pattern or print, whereas intricately seamed designs are better made up in a plain fabric. Checks and stripes are more difficult to work with as they have to be matched with great care if the end product is to look effective so choose a style with few seams.

Cotton fabrics, in whatever form, whether tough like denim and poplin or fine like lawn and cambric, are easy to cut, sew and handle. Use a mercerised sewing thread and a needle suitable to the thickness of the fabric. A needle which is too thick will result in an ugly row of holes along the stitching line.

Woollen fabrics need lining as they tend to lose shape easily. Sew with a pure silk or mercerised thread and a needle to suit the fabric.

Synthetic fabrics are generally easy to sew, using a synthetic thread to-

Right. *A beautifully made checked jacket with seam and pocket lines exactly matching.*

Fabric	Fibre	Thread	Needle sizes Hand-sewing	Machine	Stitches per inch
Fine such as lawn, georgette, voile, chiffon, organdie, net, lace	synthetic and mixtures cotton and linen wool silk	synthetic 60 mercerised 50 mercerised 50 or silk silk	9 9 9 9	9 to 11 9 to 11 9 to 11 9 to 11	12 to 15 12 to 16 12 to 16 12 to 14
Light-weight such as poplin, gingham silk, cotton	synthetic and mixtures cotton and linen wool silk	synthetic 60 mercerised 50 mercerised 50 or silk silk	8–9 8–9 8–9 8–9	11 to 14 11 to 14 11 to 14 11 to 14	12 to 15 12 to 15 12 to 15 12 to 15
Medium-weight such as gabardine, brocade, tweed, water proofed	synthetic and mixtures cotton linen wool silk	synthetic 60 mercerised 50 mercerised 40 mercerised 50 or silk silk	8–9 7–8 7–8 7–8 7–8	11 to 14 11 to 14 11 to 14 11 to 14 11 to 14	10 to 12 12 to 15 12 to 14 12 to 14 12 to 14
Heavy-weight such as coatings, canvas, heavy furnishing fabrics	synthetic and mixtures cotton linen wool silk	synthetic 40 mercerised 40 mercerised 40 mercerised 40 or silk silk	6 7–8 6–7 7–8 7–8	16 to 18 14 to 16 14 to 16 14 to 16 14 to 16	10 to 12 10 to 12 10 to 12 10 to 12 10 to 12
Some special fabrics velvet	synthetic and mixtures cotton silk	synthetic 60 mercerised 50 silk	8–9 7–8 7–8	11 to 14 11 to 14 11 to 14	10 to 12 10 to 12 10 to 12
fine leather and PVC		synthetic 40		14 to 18	8 to 10

gether with a fine or a ball-point needle. Some woven synthetics fray so allow extra seam allowance when cutting and handle the fabric carefully while sewing it. It is easier to sew synthetics or any flimsy fabric on the machine if a piece of tissue paper is placed under the fabric and the stitching worked through all thicknesses. This adds bulk and allows the machine to get a grip on the fabric. After the seam has been sewn, tear the paper away.

Jersey fabrics should have all the pattern pieces cut lengthways with the grain. If the jersey has been pulled out of line, cut the edge straight first and be careful not to stretch the fabric while cutting out the pattern and making up. Make open seams and, to prevent the seam allowance curling, loop-stitch it by hand. Sew with a pure silk or synthetic thread, either of which will 'give' with the fabric. Use a small zig-zag or stretch stitch on the machine, with about twelve stitches to the inch.

Velvet should have all pattern pieces cut with the pile running in the same direction. Make open seams and reduce the bulk of the fabric by trimming the seams narrowly and by slitting the darts open. Use silk or synthetic thread and a fine needle on the machine. Make twelve to fifteen stitches to the inch.

Lace seam allowances must be trimmed narrowly or they will show through the fine fabric. Machine with a small, close stitch.

Brocade frays badly so cut out and fit pattern pieces from the lining fabric first. When sewing the brocade, leave a large seam allowance to allow for fraying and oversew this immediately by hand or machine. Stay-stitch curves to prevent any stretching. Use a small stitch with a fine machine needle.

Chiffon must be cut with care. Use really sharp shears and cut out on a non-slippery surface. Sew with a fine needle, making French seams and hand-rolled hems, as these are least likely to show through the fabric. Hand-sewing is best if the fabric proves difficult to work with.

Altering paper patterns

Although there are a variety of pattern sizes available, most designs do need slight adjustments to ensure a perfect fit. It is important to have your own proportions measured accurately before cutting out.

Tie a tape around the waist to define the waistline and then measure as follows.

Bust: around the fullest part of the bust in front, raising the tape measure so that it passes just below the shoulder blades at the back.

Hips: around the widest part of the hips usually 18 to 20.5cm (7 to 8in) below the waist.

Waist: around the natural waistline.

Back length: from the nape of the neck to the waistline.

Front length: from the base of the neck at the top of the shoulder line, down over the fullest part of the bust to the waistline.

Shoulder: from the base of the neck to the crown of the shoulder.

Sleeve: from the crown of the shoulder to the elbow and from the elbow to the wrist with the arm bent.

Patterns are usually bought to correspond to the individual bust size and alterations, if necessary, are then made to the pattern at the hips but, if you are of a small build with a largish bust, purchase a smaller pattern instead and allow for a larger bust in the pattern alteration.

The best method of testing a pattern, with the exception of the sleeve pieces, is to pin up one half and try it on in order to determine the length in relation to the figure. To test the sleeve pattern, which would tear if pinned up for fitting, take the outer arm measurement from shoulder to elbow and down to the wrist, with the arm bent and compare this measurement with the pattern, taking into account any extra style fullness. If there are a lot of adjustments to be made, it is worthwhile testing the pattern in cotton or calico first, and using this as the basic pattern.

Never cut the pattern pieces to the actual body measurements, as all pattern manufacturers allow for ease in their patterns and this ease must be allowed for when the pattern is adapted.

When making major alterations to a pattern try to preserve the proportion

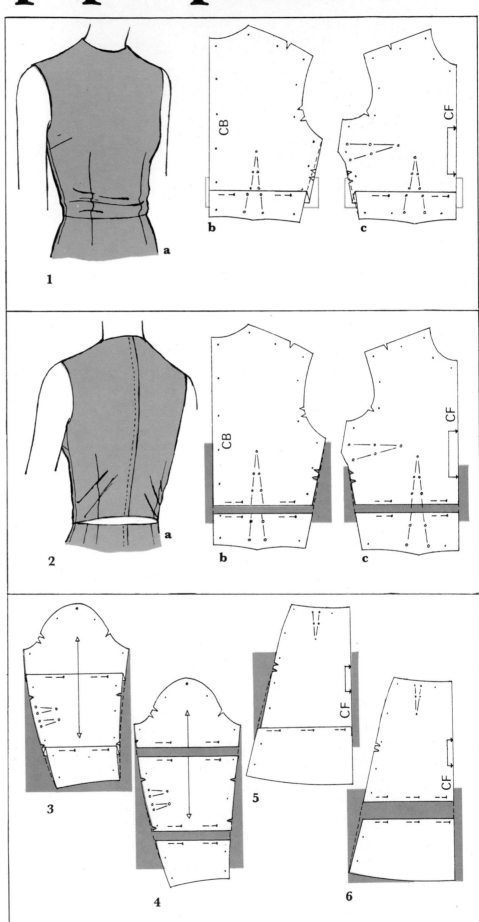

of the pattern and disturb the outline
as little as possible. Always keep in mind
that an alteration to one part of a
garment affects the pieces adjacent to it.
Try to make all alterations which en-
tail an addition to the pattern before
the garment is cut out, while an
alteration which diminishes the pattern
can be made later.

Shortening and lengthening

When shortening or lengthening a garment, try to keep all the main lines of
the pattern intact.
A bodice which is too long (Fig. 1a), will
crease above the waistline. To shorten,
make horizontal tucks on the pattern,
pin it down onto paper and straighten
the seam lines (Fig. 1b and c).
If the bodice is too short, creases will
form at the side seams and the bodice
will ride above the waistline (Fig. 2a).
To lengthen, crease and cut across the
pattern horizontally. Spread it by the
required amount and pin the pattern to
paper. Straighten the seam lines (Fig.
2b and c).
If the sleeve piece is too long (Fig.3),
make horizontal tucks on the pattern
and pin it down onto paper. If the
sleeve is to short (Fig. 4), crease and cut
across the pattern horizontally. Spread
by the required amount and pin the
pattern onto paper.
Skirts: To shorten, make a horizontal
tuck on the pattern and pin it down
onto paper (Fig. 5). To lengthen,
crease and cut across the pattern horizontally. Spread by the required a-
mount and pin the pattern onto paper
(Fig. 6).

More complex alteration.

Square shoulders: cause creasing
across the neckline (Fig. 7a). Remedy by
pinning the bodice onto paper to armhole level. Cut the new shoulder line
allowing the required amount 1.3 to
2cm ($\frac{1}{2}$ to $\frac{3}{4}$in) at the armhole, tapering
down to nothing at the neck (Fig.7b and
c). Raise the line at the underarm to
maintain the original size of the armhole (7d and e). Often, however, this
type of figure requires a larger armhole,
in which case omit the addition at the
underarm and increase the sleeve head
to make it fit into the larger armhole
with the correct amount of ease (Fig.7f).

Sloping shoulders: cause folds at the
armhole (Fig. 8a). Draw a line from the
armhole tapering down to nothing at
the neckline and cut away the required
amount (Fig. 8b and c). Cut away the
same amount at the underarm to retain
the original armhole size and sleeve
head (Fig. 8d and e). This type of

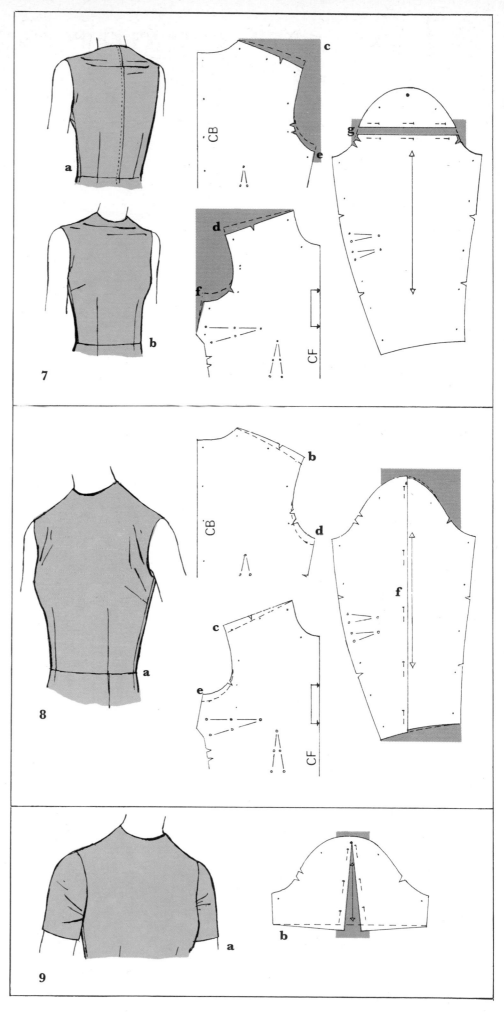

7

8

9

7

figure often has thin arms so it may be necessary to decrease the sleeve width by making a lengthwise fold down the centre of the sleeve (Fig. 8f). There is no need to cut away at the bodice underarm.

Large upper arm: causes creases at the underarm and across the crown of the sleeve (Fig. 9a). Slash the pattern through the centre from the hem to the top of the crown. Pin the pattern to a sheet of paper spreading the pattern pieces apart by the required amount. Draw around the spread out pattern to give the new sleeve shape (Fig. 9b).

Round shoulders: cause the neckline and collar to stand away from the back neck (Fig. 10a). Slash the pattern about 11.5cm (4½in) down from the neck at the centre back to the armhole. Do not cut away (Fig. 10b). Raise the neck to the required amount 2 to 2.5cm (¾ to 1in) and pin onto paper (Fig 10c). Restore the neck to its original measurement, using the lengthened, curved line if the design has a centre back seam (Fig. 10d), or the straight line if the pattern is cut to a fold (Fig. 10e), taking the extra fullness into the dart at the neckline (Fig. 10f). Alternatively, slash across from the centre back to the armhole, then slash down from the centre of the shoulder. Raise the back neck and spread the shoulder to make a shoulder dart (Fig. 10g).

Hollow back: causes horizontal wrinkles below the waist (Fig. 11a). On the back skirt pattern, cut away about 2cm (¾in) from the centre back, sloping to nothing at the side seam (Fig. 11b).

Large waist: Where it is not practicable to alter the side seams, increase the front waist measurement, slash the skirt pattern down from the centre of the waistline and across the side seam at approximately hip level. Spread the pattern to give the required amount at the waist and pin onto paper (Fig. 12).

High abdomen: causes the skirt to kick up at the hem and the skirt to crease horizontally around hip level (Fig 13a). Slash down from the centre front line of the pattern at approximately hip level. Do not cut away. Spread the section towards the centre front to give extra width and height. Redraw the waistline and centre front line to straighten it (Fig. 13b).

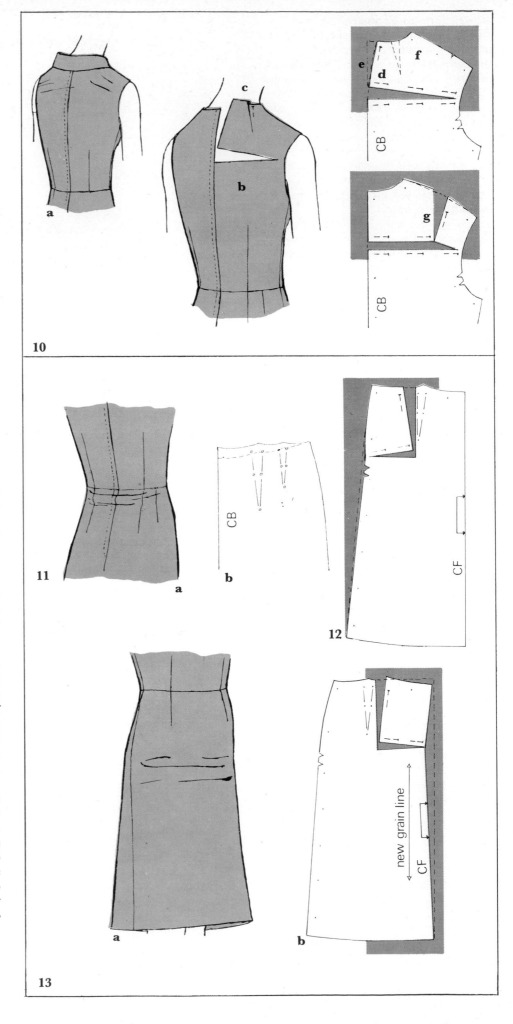

Alterations to Trousers

Trousers usually create special fitting problems because of the complexity of the proportions involved. Take the hip measurement when choosing the pattern and make all lengthwise adjustments (that is crotch and trouser lengths) first.

To determine crotch length, sit on a firm chair and measure from the waistline to the seat (Fig. 1). To double check this important measurement, measure from the centre front waistline, down under the crotch and up to the centre back waist. Add ease to this measurement in the proportion of 1.3 cm ($\frac{1}{2}$in) if the hips are less than 89cm (35in), 2cm ($\frac{3}{4}$in) if the hips are 89cm (35in) to 96.5cm (38in) and 2.5cm (1in) if the hip measurement is more than 96.5cm (38in).

To adjust the length of the crotch: draw a line across the pattern at right angles to the grain line from the widest part of the crotch to the side seam. The length of the pattern from the waistline to this line should be the same as the crotch length plus the ease allowance.

If the pattern is too long crease along the shortening line and fold a tuck to take up the desired amount (Fig. 2). Tape in place and re-draw the seams and construction markings to retain the original shape of the side seam. If too short, cut along the lengthening line (Fig. 3) and open the pattern to the desired amount. Insert a piece of paper behind this section and tape in place. Re-draw the seams and construction markings to retain the original shape of the side and crotch seams. Remember to make the same adjustment to the front and back pattern pieces.

For adjustments to trouser length: measure the length of the pattern from the waistline to the lower edge. This should be the same as the measurement from the waist to ankle. If the pattern is too short or too long, use the same principle as above to correct this (Figs. 2 and 3). Make sure that there is adequate length for the hem allowance and for turn-ups if these are required.

Hip line adjustments: on the average figure the hip line is measured approximately 20.5cm (8in) below the waistline. Draw a horizontal line on the pattern this distance from the waist.

Take the hip measurement on the pattern at the hip line. There should be 5cm (2in) ease allowance. If the pattern does not measure 5cm (2in) more than the body measurement, the pattern will

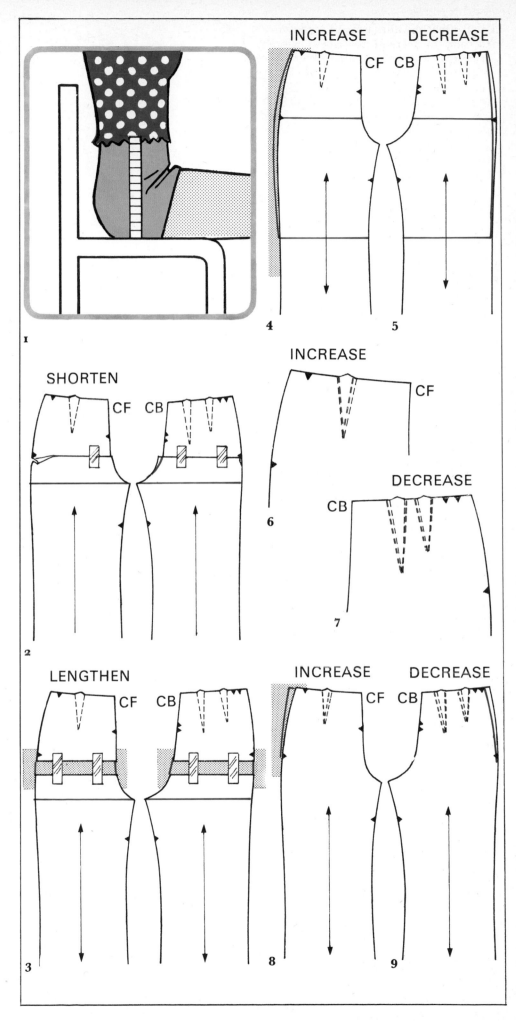

need adjusting. To increase, determine the amount needed, divide this total by four and increase each side seam by this amount. Measure the amount of adjustment out from the hip line edge at the side seam on both front and back pieces and mark. Tape a piece of tissue underneath each pattern section Taper from the original cutting line both above the knee and at the waistline, retaining the shape of the leg and the width of the waist (Fig. 4).

To decrease use the same principle but subtract the amount at the side seams (Fig. 5).

The waistline: the ease allowance should be 1.3cm (½in) to 2cm (¾in). The waistline can be increased or decreased by adjusting the darts. Each dart can be increased or decreased by as much as 0.6cm (¼in) but no more (Figs. 6 and 7).

If this is not sufficient the side seams can also be altered. Divide the amount of increase or decrease by four and adjust each side seam edge by this amount. Taper to the hipline, being careful not to change the hip measurement (Figs. 8 and 9).

To adjust the width of the lower edge: determine the amount to be added or subtracted and divide by four. Alter the side and inside seams accordingly (Figs. 10 and 11).

To adjust the width of the leg: add or subtract to the front and back inside leg seams at the crotch point, tapering the line to the lower edge of the pattern. Do not add to the side seams but add more width to the crotch instead (Fig. 12).

To accommodate thin thighs, decrease both front and back inside leg seams at crotch point and taper to the lower edge of the pattern (Fig. 13).

Unusual alterations
Sway back: this will cause folds in the trousers below the back waist.

Eliminate these by removing the extra fullness at the centre back. Slash straight across the back to the side seam about 9cm (3½in) below the waistline. Overlap the slash line to remove the necessary amount. Re-draw the centre back seam and also the darts if they have been affected. The back waistline will thus have been decreased (Fig. 14a and b).

If the normal waistline width is required, add the amount trimmed from the centre back to side seam and taper from the waist to the hipline (Fig. 15).

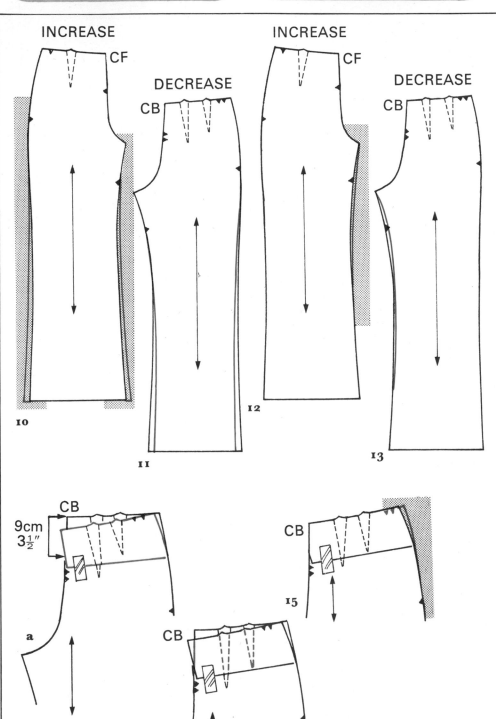

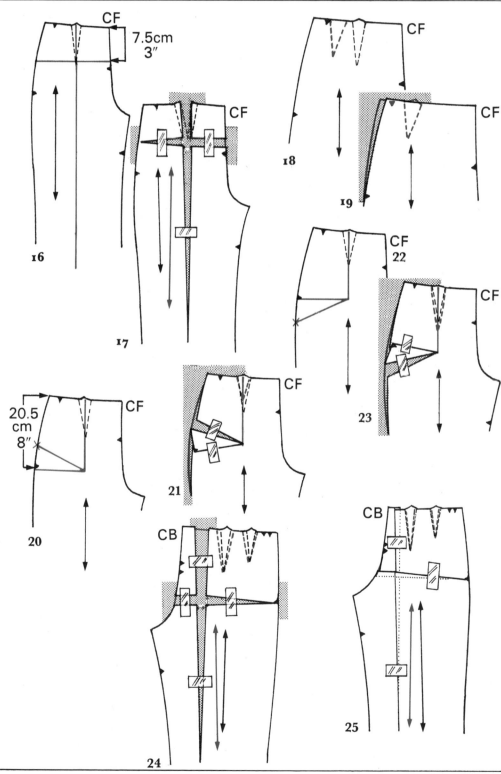

Large stomach: draw a line through the centre of the waistline dart to the knee. This line should be parallel to the grainline.

Then draw a horizontal line from the centre front to the side seam about 7.5cm (3in) below the waistline (Fig. 16). Slash the horizontal line to the side seam and open the pattern a quarter of the amount required. Slash the vertical line and open the pattern a quarter of the amount required, keeping the centre front straight. Insert a piece of tissue under the slashes and tape in position. Adjust the waistline dart in the middle of the slash, returning it to its original position and size (Fig. 17).

Protruding hips: extra dart fullness released at the point of the hip bones will solve this problem. The larger dart releases more fullness. Re-position and increase the width of the dart so that it is in line with the hip bone. For some figures the dart may need shortening (Fig. 18). As a result, the waistline becomes smaller, so add the difference to the side seam and taper to the hip-line (Fig. 19).

One hip higher than the natural hipline: measure 20.5cm (8in) from the waistline and draw a line through the centre of the dart keeping in line with the straight grain. Square across at the hipline to the vertical line. At the side seam where the hip is higher, measure down from the waistline to the hip bone and mark. Draw a line from this mark to the point where the vertical and horizontal meet (Fig. 20). Slash along this line and the horizontal line and overlap the pattern. This will open the pattern at the new hip line. Adjust the amount, overlapping to fit the hip and tape in place. Re-draw the side seam from the waistline, tapering to the new hipline.

Make this adjustment to both front and back pattern pieces. The dart will then need shortening to the level of the new hipline (Fig. 21).

One hip lower than the natural hip-line: having drawn the vertical and horizontal as above, measure down from the horizontal to the new hipline and mark. Draw a line from this mark to the point at which the vertical and horizontal lines meet (Fig. 22). Slash along this line and the horizontal line and overlap the pattern. This will open the pattern at the new hipline. Adjust the amount, overlapping to fit the hip and tape in place. Re-draw the side seam from waistline, taper to the hip (Fig. 23).

Large seat: width and length at the fullest part of the seat must be increased. Determine the amount of increase necessary for the adjustment. Slash the pattern vertically to the knee, between the centre back and the back dart, parallel to the grain line. Measure 20.5cm (8in) below the waistline and slash the pattern horizontally from the centre back to the side seam. Open the vertical and horizontal slashes each to a quarter of the amount required, keeping the centre back straight. Insert a piece of tissue and tape in place. Redraw the cutting lines. If the waistline becomes too large, divide the adjustment equally between the back darts and increase each one (Fig. 24).

Flat seat: as above but instead of opening the vertical and horizontal slashes, overlap them each by a quarter of the amount required. If the waistline becomes too small, divide the vertical adjustment equally between all the back darts and decrease them by this amount (Fig. 25).

Right. *Two different styles of trousers made up from a single pattern adapted to fit each individual figure type.*

A final tip on fitting trousers

After the pattern pieces have been cut out in the fabric and marked, fold each piece vertically in half with the wrong sides together. Press in the creases firmly. The front crease points to the first dart or pleat, and the back crease stops at the crotch seam.

During the first fitting, ensure that the creases hang straight. If a crease hangs inwards, raise the trousers at the waistline on the appropriate side until the crease hangs correctly. This occurs because the two hips are not exactly the same (Fig. 26).

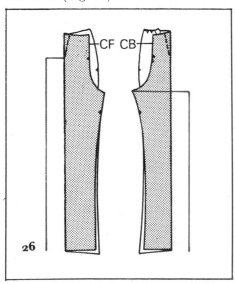

Cutting out

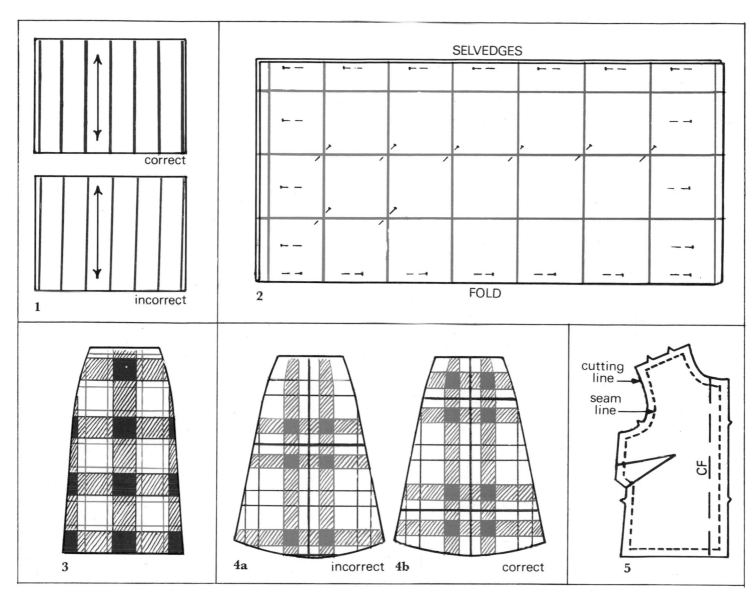

1 correct / incorrect

2 SELVEDGES / FOLD

3

4a incorrect **4b** correct

5 cutting line / seam line / CF

To make cutting out a pleasure, it is necessary to have a large working surface at a comfortable height. A large table or a wide wooden board that can be rested on the top of a chest of drawers, bed or table should be used.

Preparations before cutting out
Unless a fabric is guaranteed shrunk when purchased, it must be shrunk before cutting out so allow for this when deciding on yardage. Allow 8 to 10cm (3 to 4in) for every metre (yard) of the fabric. To shrink the fabric, take a piece of clean, unbleached calico the width of the fabric and half its length. Soak the calico in water and wring out. Place the fabric, wrong side up and opened out to its full width, on a large table. Place the calico on it and smooth

it out so that there are no wrinkles in it. Snip the selvedges of the fabric every 5 to 8cm (2 to 3in). Fold up the rest of the fabric over the calico to make a sandwich of fabric with calico in between. Roll up the whole sandwich tightly, wrap it up in paper and leave it overnight. Gradually unroll the fabric over an ironing board and iron it on the wrong side until it is completely dry. Move the iron smoothly to prevent the impression of the iron being left on the fabric.

To cut
Fold the fabric with selvedges together and the grain running lengthways and place all pattern pieces to be cut on the fold in position first. Place the other main pattern pieces on the material,

checking that the grain lines are straight by measuring in from the edge of the fabric. Secure the pattern with one or two pins until all pieces are laid out and, where some pattern pieces have to be cut out twice, mark around them with chalk and then re-pin them elsewhere on the fabric.

Interlock the pattern pieces, wherever possible, to make the best economical use of the material, such as at armholes, for example.

Special care should be taken with fabric designs which need to be matched at seams or at the centre front and extra material should be allowed for matching up when buying. When working with plaids and stripes find the dominant lines, in plaids one runs horizontally and one vertically, and ensure the pattern is

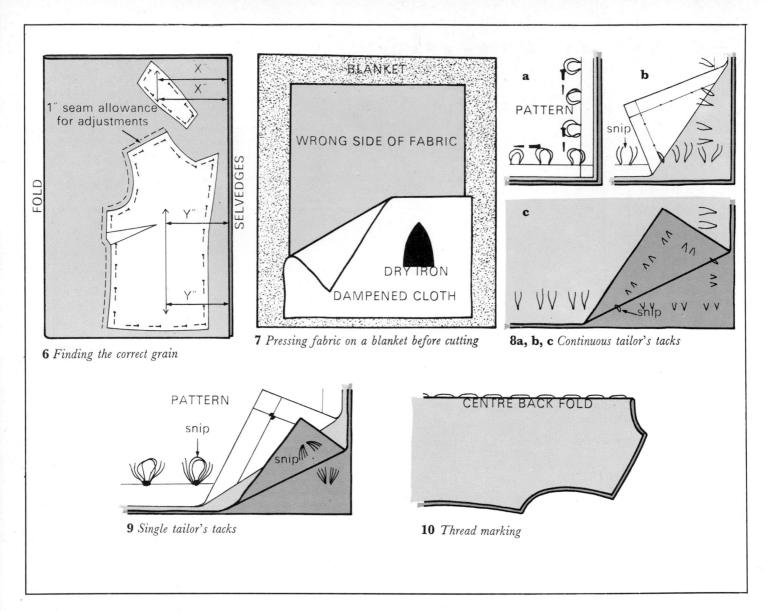

6 *Finding the correct grain*

7 *Pressing fabric on a blanket before cutting*

8a, b, c *Continuous tailor's tacks*

9 *Single tailor's tacks*

10 *Thread marking*

printed in line with the grain. Fold the fabric so that the fold is either on the centre of a design or on a dominant line (Fig. 1). Pin along the selvedges (Fig. 2) and across the ends matching the design every 5cm (2in). Then pin at intervals all over the fabric to see that the pattern matches exactly. For skirts with a straight hem the dominant line should fall at the hem (Fig. 3). For a curved hemline the dominant line should fall above the hemline (Fig. 4). The dominant line should never fall across the widest part of the garment. Also remember to match the seam lines and not the cutting line (Fig. 5). With floral designs the stems should always, if possible, point downwards.

Pattern pieces are generally cut from double fabric but when a design has to be matched at the seams it is best to cut the adjoining pieces from single fabric to ensure matching the design. Take care, when handling velvet or a similar fabrics where each pattern piece must be cut with the pile or nap running downwards. Leave pieces to be cut from single fabric until all others have been cut but make sure that there is sufficient fabric before cutting out.

When the general layout has been checked, pin each pattern piece to the fabric with the pins placed vertical to the cutting line but not over it, so that the scissors will not cut over the pins and thereby give a rough edge. On fabrics that are liable to be marked with the pins, use fine sewing needles instead. Cut, using a large pair of scissors with long blades, making as few cuts as possible to ensure a smooth edge. Move around the pattern pieces on the table rather than moving the fabric.

Pattern markings

Transfer all pattern markings onto the fabric using tailor's tacks and thread markings before removing the paper patterns.

Always cut notches out into spare fabric and not into the seam allowance as this must be left intact for making strong seams, especially on fraying

fabrics.

Mark all stitching lines with continuous tailor's tacks (Fig. 8) making equal-length, equally spaced stitches in double tacking thread through the pattern and both layers of fabric, making a loop at each stitch. Snip through the centre of the loop, unpin the pattern and gently ease the paper away. Pull the fabric edges apart gently and cut the stitches, leaving tufts on both sides.

For marking style details, such as darts, buttonholes and pocket positions, use a contrast colour double thread and take a stitch through the dot or hole in the paper pattern and through both layers of fabric (Fig. 9). Repeat, leaving a loop. Snip through the centre of the thread loop and then gently remove the paper pattern.

For marking centre back lines, centre front lines, pleats and other lines that need to be accurate and absolutely straight, make a single row of stitches through one layer of the fabric only using yet another colour tacking thread (Fig. 10).

Seams, stitches and finishes

Each type of garment, depending on fabric and style, will look better and wear longer if sewn with a seam that complements it. For example, if working with a thick, bulky fabric, choose a seam that involves the absolute minimum layers of fabric, whereas a thinner fabric, or one that tends to fray, should have an enclosed or a double-stitched seam. Knowing how to sew various seams, and when to use them, will help to achieve that look of perfection.

Tension

Before starting any actual stitching, check that the tension and foot presure on the sewing machine are correct for the particular thread and fabric being used. Do this by cutting two 4cm (1½in) wide strips of fabric, each about 20cm (8in) long and place them one on top of the other. Sew a straight seam down the middle of the strips. If the bottom strip ends up shorter than the top one, the tension on the pressure foot is too great. Reduce the tension and try the seam again until the sewn strips are the same length. If the top strip is shorter than the bottom one, she problem is reversed, and the tension needs tightening. The stitches on the top and the reverse of the seam should look identical. If the reverse stitches look tight, loosen the top tension, if they are loose, tighten the top tension. The spool case tension rarely needs adjustment (Fig. 1).

Joining seams

The most widely used joining method is the plain or open seam, but some garments and types of fabric need certain seams reinforced and some are better with a stronger seam. Then, when all seams are joined (and any reinforcing and neatening completed), comes the finishing: the hems to be turned up, the buttonholes to be worked and any fancy, decorative stitching to be added. Each has a stitch that is best for the job.

Preparation

Tacking is the first essential for a good final result. This secures the pieces of the garment together in their correct positions for seaming and also for the first fitting, when any necessary altera-

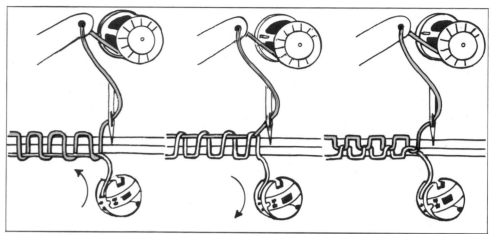

1 *Finding the correct tension*

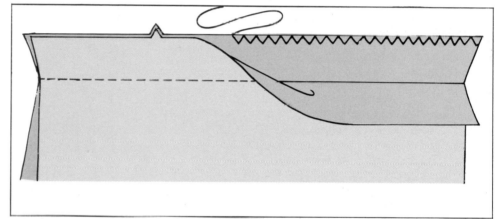

2 *Plain or open seam*   **3** *French seam*

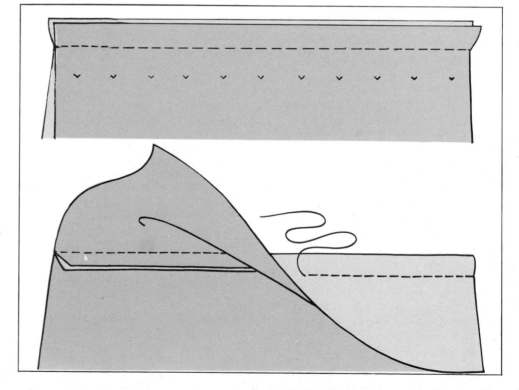

15

tions can be made with no problems. For stitching use double tacking thread, which is weak and easily broken for removal after the actual seams are sewn. Work on a flat surface. Make a knot at the end of the thread and take one long stitch, leave an equal space, then make a stitch half the length of the first. Work alternately like this until the end of the seam and finish off with a double back stitch. This tacking seam is stronger than having all the stitches the same length so it is the most useful one for fitting purposes.

Seam types

Plain or open seam. This is the most generally used seam in dressmaking as it gives a perfectly flat finish. It may be used on all skirt, bodice and sleeve seams, except on the most transparent of fabrics and is worked as follows.

Pin the two pieces of fabric with right sides together, raw edges level and matching notches. Tack on the seam line and stitch the depth of the seam allowance away from the raw edge. Press the seam open and overcast the raw edges by hand or machine to strengthen the seam against fraying and wear (Fig. 2).

French seam. This is often used on flimsy fabrics because it is stronger and neater with no untidy edges to show through transparent fabrics. With wrong sides together and raw edges level, tack and stitch 0.3 to 0.6cm ($\frac{1}{8}$ to $\frac{1}{4}$in) outside the stitching line (taking the larger measurement if the fabric is likely to fray.) Remove the tacking stitches and press the seam open. Trim the raw edges of the seam neatly, then fold the fabric so that the right sides are together. Roll the seam until the join is at the edge, then tack and stitch the seam again, using the machine foot as a guide to keep the seam an even width. Make sure that the raw edges are encased (Fig. 3).

Neatening seams

With fabrics that are likely to fray, take a larger seam allowance and protect the raw edges with a stronger stitch such as loop stitch, or zig-zag stitch on the machine. On badly fraying fabrics bind the seam, using Paris binding for seams cut with the straight of the grain and bias binding for seams cut on the cross.

Bindings

Braids for binding are many and varied, depending on the job they have to do. For example, wide, woollen-woven braids are suitable mainly for edging single-layer garments in firm fabrics,

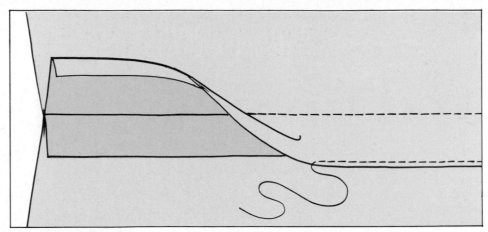

4 *Flat fell seam*

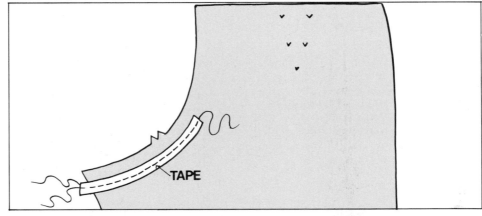

5 *Loop stitch*

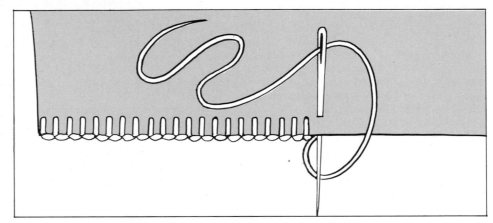

6 *Strengthening the seam*

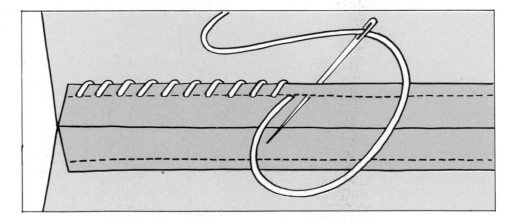

7 *Overcasting*

such as heavy velours or reversible garments, where no facings are needed. Narrower artificial silk braids are used in a variety of ways: for edging raw edges or for finishing off seams inside the garment. Narrow braids of less than 2.5cm (1in) wide are not really suitable for edging as, when they are turned over and are therefore half their original width, they are too narrow unless the fabric is very fine indeed. Braids are also a good way of adding a decorative touch to a garment. When binding, it is important to remember that the edge that will be seen should be stitched on first.

With straight binding, pin the braid 1cm ($\frac{3}{8}$in) from the raw edge of the garment, leaving 1.3cm ($\frac{1}{2}$in) at the end to neaten afterwards. If you have to turn a corner, leave a loop so that you can mitre the braid. Turn in the end of the braid then stitch down one long edge. Turn the braid over the raw edge of the garment and hand-sew the edge of the braid to the garment with small, firm, felling stitches. Mitre the corner. Edging with bias binding again needs care: pin, tack and sew the turned in edge to the edge of the garment, then take the other edge over, without disturbing the fold edge of the side already sewn and hand-sew the fold edge to the inside of the garment with neat felling stitches.

Flat fell seams: For a superbly neat finish inside the garment. Trim one side of the seam allowance to 0.3 to 0.6cm ($\frac{1}{8}$ to $\frac{1}{4}$in), press the other side of the seam allowance over it, turn in the raw edge narrowly and stitch along it to cover the smaller raw edge (Fig. 4).

Loop stitch: used for neatening and decorative work, is often confused with blanket stitch or buttonhole stitch. Loop stitch is worked from left to right over a raw or a folded edge. The thread loops under the needle as the stitch is formed (Fig. 5). The effect can be compared with buttonhole stitch described in the chapter on buttonholes.

Reinforcement stitching
Stay stitching: This is a row of machine stitching worked just outside the seam line, nearer to the raw edge, to prevent stretching of the fabric. It is used, for example, if the pattern pieces are cut on the cross (a V neckline or the waist of a skirt cut on the bias) or where the weight of the fabric is liable to make the garment lose its shape or if the fabric is very loosely woven.
Certain seams, such as underarm seams,

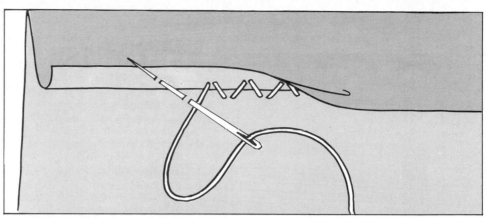

8 *Invisible hemming*

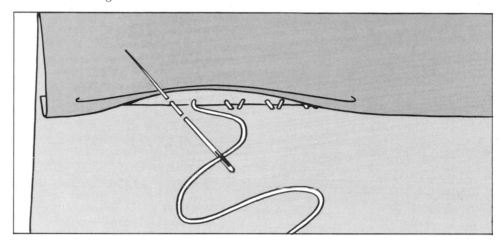

9 *Hemming*

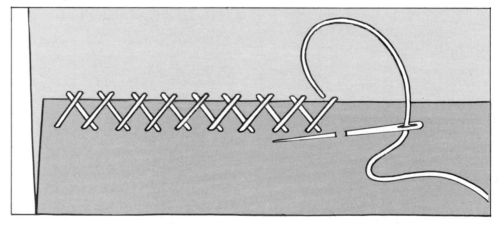

10 *Herringbone stitch*

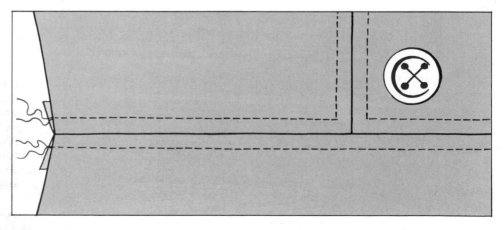

11 *Topstitching*

the crotch of trousers or shorts are subject to additional strain and therefore need to be strengthened. Cut a piece of tape and stitch it into the seam as it is being sewn (Fig. 6). For raglan sleeves, most of which are cut on the bias, sew in a piece of tape which has already been shrunk to prevent the seam from losing its shape. Where a row of pleats is to receive a great deal of strain, stitch a length of tape across the top of them, on the wrong side. Shaped seams often need clipping right down to the stitching line, so reinforce curves before clipping, either by working a row of machine stitching or by sewing a length of tape on the stitching line. Do not clip through the tape.

Finishing stitches

Overcasting is worked over the raw edge of seams on fabrics that are likely to fray. On loosely woven or stretched fabrics sew a row of machine stitching first as this will hold the edge firmly while the overcasting is being worked over it. Trim the edge close to the machine stitching in stages before overcasting (Fig. 7).

Bar tacks are made to strengthen the top of a pleat or opening and are decorative as well as functional. Make a neat bar of four stitches, then loop-stitch tightly across the strands along the length of the bar.

Slipstitching is worked by hand to join two folded edges such as ends of belts and front hem edges of blouses, jackets or coats. Take a small amount of fabric in the fold at one edge, then take a similar amount from the other edge and pull the thread fairly tightly.

Invisible hemming is a relatively new and excellent method of hemming which can be worked on most fabrics to perfection. It is not suitable for finer fabrics such as cotton or voile. Mark the hem line. Turn the hem up and tack close to the fold line. Press the fold line only. Trim the hem allowance evenly to the required depth and neaten the raw edge by overcasting by hand or machine. Sew the hem to the garment by picking up one thread of the fabric alternately on the garment and hem 0.6cm ($\frac{1}{4}$in) below the raw edge of the hem allowance at 0.6cm to 1cm intervals, depending on the weight of the fabric. The stitches must not show on the right side of the garment, nor must they be pulled tight (Fig. 8).

Hemming stitch is used for sewing hems on thinner fabrics and is always worked over a folded edge. Hemming is worked from right to left using evenly sized and evenly spaced stitches which should be as close and short as the

fabric will allow. The correct angle of the needle for this stitch is 45° and, unless the needle is held accurately, the stitches will be uneven and irregular (Fig. 9).

Herringbone stitch is used not only as a neatening stitch for inside seam edges but also as a finishing stitch when turning up hems on thick materials. It is worked from left to right of the garment over a raw or folded edge. Hold the work as flat as possible and pick up very small amounts of fabric in the hem itself and then in the material above it. Leave the stitches loose or they will make a ridge on the right side of the fabric (Fig. 10).

Topstitching is used as a decorative effect and is worked on the right side of the garment to accentuate a definite line in the design. It is often sewn in a stronger thread such as buttonhole twist for more emphasis. In this case it is worked from the wrong side of the buttonhole. Use a large stitch so that the needle will go through the thicker fabric. Make sure that the seam allowance of any seams to be topstitched is sewn flat on the inside and topstitch on both sides of the seam (Fig. 11).

Above. *Contrasting topstitching used to emphasize the line of this simple dress.*

Linings, interlinings and interfacings

Lining is extremely important for, however well the garment is made, it will not last long, nor will it hang properly if it is not well lined. It will soon fall out of shape if it has not the added body and support provided not only by a lining but, in some cases, an interlining and interfacing or stiffening as well.

Linings

A garment is usually lined for three reasons: to give substance and support to the main fabric, to add warmth and to enhance the appearance of the garment, either when the inside is exposed (for example, when coats and jackets fall open at the front) or so that one cannot see through a transparent fabric. Most garments look better for a lining, which improves the 'hang' and also lengthens wear, as it saves the cloth from a certain amount of friction.

Lining materials

The lining should complement the garment so purchase fabric and lining at the same time. Tafetta is ideal when a stiff effect is essential and satin or crepe when a clinging one is aimed for. Satin is a smooth, soft and inexpensive lining, good for most weights of cloth but avoid a cheap one if it is to line a garment that is to receive a good deal of wear. A cheap lining will tear and disintegrate and will have to be replaced by a new one. Jap silk is a good thin and soft lining but it is expensive. Bemberg is equally effective and is less expensive. Satin-backed crepe is suitable for heavier tweeds and Milium is a satin-weave backed with aluminium which is used for extra warmth with winter coats and jackets. If using Milium as a lining, an interlining would not be needed

Choose a washable lining if the main fabric is washable. If the top fabric is dry cleanable, choose a dry cleanable, lining. The lining should have the same pressing temperature as the top fabric.

There are two main methods of sewing in a lining.

Separate lining. The top fabric garment and the lining are almost completely made up. The wrong side of the

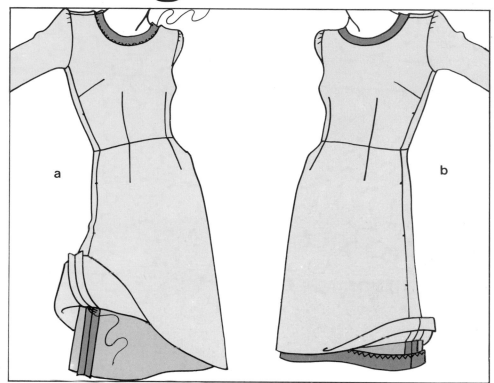

1 *Separate lining*

2 *Mounting*

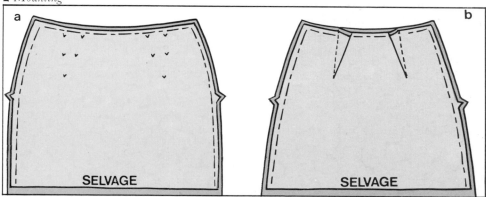

3 *Lining a skirt*

lining then is placed to the wrong side of the top fabric garment and joined to the neckline seam (and waist if there is one) (Fig. 1a). A loose dress lining can also be attached to the side seams of the garment, with 1.5cm (½in) bar tacks, worked at 20cm (8in) intervals. The lining should, in this case, be slightly looser than the fabric garment. Mark all darts and pattern details on the lining pieces as well as on the top fabric. Turn up the hem of the lining slightly more than the hem of the garment so that it is not visible when the garment is being worn (Fig. 1b).

Mounting method, backing or underlining. The lining is cut out in exactly the same way as the top fabric, each lining piece is placed with its top fabric piece, wrong sides together, and tacked (Fig. 2a). It is then treated as if it were one pattern piece. Starting from

Interfacings	
Outside fabric	**correct interfacing**
Dress weight: cotton linen wool	pre-shrunk treated lawn iron-on or non-woven interfacing as recommended by the manufacturer
Suit-weight: cotton linen wool	treated cotton interfacing, such as bleached calico iron-on or non-woven interfacing as recommended by the manufacturer
Man-made fibre fabrics	non-woven interfacing as recommended by the manufacturer for very light fabrics (lawn, voile, etc.) pure silk or nylon organza
Pure silk	fine lawn or pure silk organza
See-through fabrics	soft organdie or pure silk organza

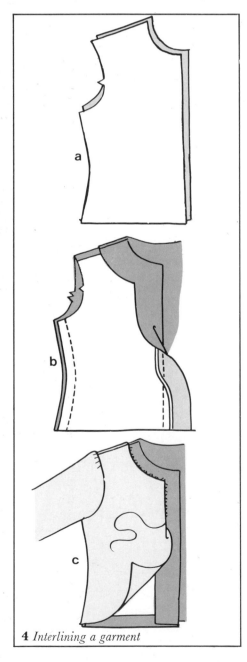

4 *Interlining a garment*

5 *Using an interlining without a seam allowance*

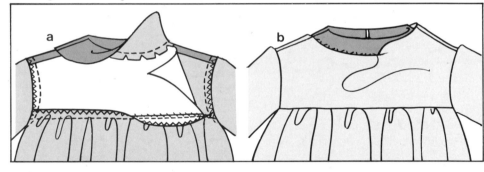

6 *Interfacing*

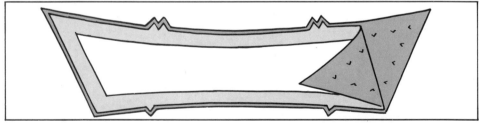

7 *Interfacing a garment with an all-in-one facing*

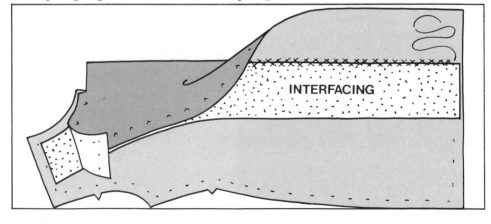

INTERFACING

the centre of each pattern piece, tack in rows up, down and across until the whole area is covered. Do not remove the tacking stitches until the whole garment is completed (Fig. 2b).

Skirts can be lined in the same way as a dress, either with the lining sewn in separately or made up together with the main fabric. Again, it can be half-lined with a short lining sewn only to the back of the skirt (Fig. 3a). Cut the lining of the skirt on the straight of the grain but lay the pattern so that the selvedge lies across the hips instead of lengthways (Fig. 3b). This is because the downward threads are stronger than the widthways ones and are thus less likely to stretch under strain in wear.

Interlinings are often sewn in to give extra body to a light-weight fabric and to prevent creasing. There are two ways of sewing in an interlining. The best way is to cut it in the same way as the fabric pieces (Fig. 4a), tack it to each respective fabric piece (Fig. 4b) and sew up the garment with interlining and fabric together, then sew in the lining afterwards in the usual way (Fig. 4c). Another method is to cut the interlining pattern without any seam allowance and, when the fabric pieces have been sewn together, place the interlining to its respective piece (Fig. 5a) and tack it to the seam allowance. Then sew in the lining (Fig. 5b).

Stiffenings and interfacings are used to give extra strength and shaping to certain parts of a garment which are subject to more stress and wear than the rest, for example collars and cuffs, behind buttonholes and facings. The iron-on facings and interfacings now available need not be cut on the cross and, indeed, need only a careful positioning of the pieces before ironing on with a warm iron. They are good for stabilising fabric, making it easier to control while sewing. Various weights are sold according to the weight of the fabric being made up and they come in two types, woven and non-woven. Make sure to choose one that matches up with the properties of the main fabric. Cut interfacings to the same shape as the pattern pieces but with no seam allowance (Fig. 6a).

With a garment that has an all-in-one facing, pin and tack the interfacing to to the wrong side of the garment with the seam allowance falling on to the facing. Sew the interfacing with the stitches in the seam allowance so that, when the facing is folded back to the inside of the garment, the stitches will not show through to the right side (Fig. 7).

Dress: Vogue Pattern No. M7723

Above. *A separate lining can be used, as shown here, to great decorative effect.*

Facings

The smallest of all pattern pieces, the facings are among the most important. Since their purpose is to ensure a good-looking finish to neckline and cuffs, front openings and collars, they can make or mar a garment.

Make sure the facing is cut in the same way as the main pattern piece that it is to back; for example, if a bodice front is to be cut on the straight of the grain, cut the front facing on the straight of the grain, too.

Remember if a pattern piece has been altered to fit individual measurements, the facing must be altered to match. Where facings have to be joined, for example a back neck facing and front facing, join them at the shoulder seams and then sew the complete facing to the garment.

An all-in-one facing

This is usually made at the front edge of a garment when a neat, straight line is required, especially on a heavy fabric where a separate facing would mean a bulky seam at the edge. The facing is simply a section of the body fabric folded back on a line indicated on the pattern piece (Fig. 1a) after any inter-linings and interfacings have been inserted (Fig. 1b). Press the folded edge.

A fitted or shaped facing

First stay-stitch the inner curved edge of the facing to give it strength and then neaten the outer edge, according to the type of fabric you are working with (Fig. 2a). For neatening, a thin fabric will just need to be turned under and slipstitched; a slightly heavier fabric can be oversewn and one that frays can be bound. With right sides together, match notches and seam lines, stitch along the seam line (Fig. 2b). Secure the end threads, grade the seam and notch the seam allowance. Turn the facing to the wrong side of the garment and roll it so that the seam comes just to the edge. Tack around the edge and press the facing to lie flat (Fig.2c). Secure the facings at seam allowances, with catchstitching.

A bias strip facing

Stay-stitch the edge of the garment to be faced. Cut a piece of fabric on the bias the desired length and width. With right sides together and beginning at a seam, tack one long edge of the bias strip to the edge of the garment it is to face (Fig. 3a). Ease the bias on in-

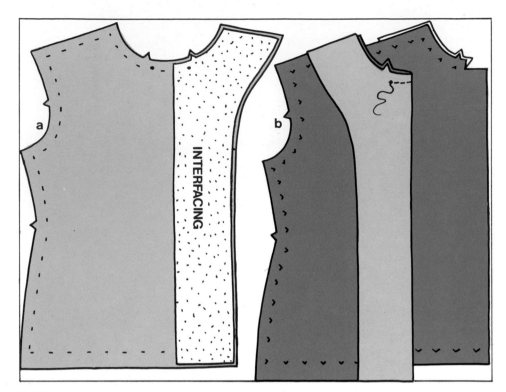

1 *All-in-one facing*

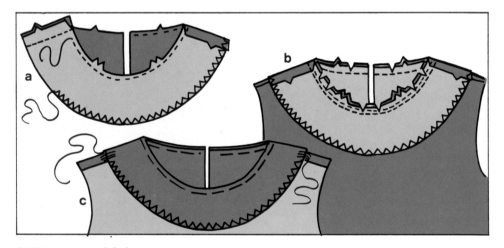

2 *Fitted or shaped facing*

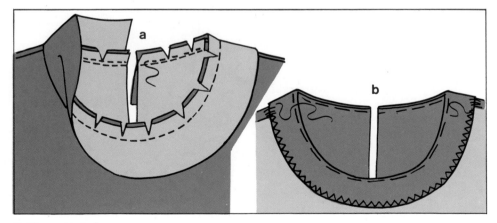

3 *Bias strip facing*

ward curves and stretch it on outer ones, so that the facing will lie flat. Press the seam open and snip into the seam allowance up to the stitching line. Turn the facing under so that the seam comes on to the edge. On the right side tack close to the folded edge and press flat. Neaten the raw edge and hem the inner edge to the inside of the garment (Fig. 3b).

Straight seam binding facing

If the edge to be faced is straight for example, the hem edge of a sleeve, topstitch a length of straight seam binding to the right side of the sleeve edge, beginning at the seam (Fig. 4a). Turn up the sleeve edge to the required length and hemstitch the binding to the wrong side of the sleeve (Fig. 4b).

Where no facing is supplied with the pattern and one is required because the style has been adapted, follow the main pattern piece taking the edge of the main pattern piece as the inner edge of the facing, and a parallel line 5cm (2in) from the inner edge as the outer edge of the facing.

When facing an outward pointing V-shape, cut a 5cm (2in) bias strip of fabric and place the facing strip along each side of the point, so that a dart may be pinned into the strip at the centre to shape it exactly to fit the angle of the point (Fig. 5a). Fold the dart to the left and stitch along the stitching line on the strip as far as the point. Then fold the dart to the right and continue stitching the other side of the point. Stitch the dart in position from the point to 0.6cm ($\frac{1}{4}$in) from the raw edge of the strip. Fold the facing over to the wrong side of the garment and finish the raw edge (Fig. 5b).

When facing an inward pointing V-shape, follow the same principle as for the outward pointing V-shape but reverse the shape of the dart (Fig. 6a). After the strip has been stitched to the garment, snip the garment seam allowance at the point nearly to the stitching line. Trim the dart, leaving a narrow seam allowance and turn the facing to the wrong side of the garment. Finish off the raw edge (Fig. 6b).

Where there is a facing along a rever, press the facing carefully to the outside of the garment as far as the point where the rever turns back and press from the inside. Any topstitching on the garment must follow the edge of the facing on the rever as far as the point where it turns back (Fig. 7a). The topstitching must be continued from just that point but on the right side of the centre front edge of the garment. (Fig. 7b).

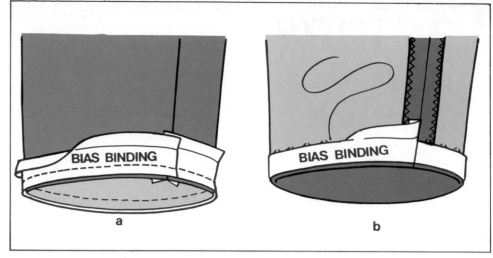

4 *Straight seam binding facing*

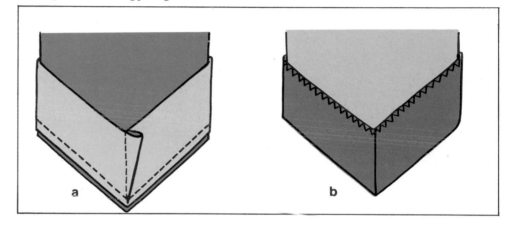

5 *Facing an outward pointing V-shape*

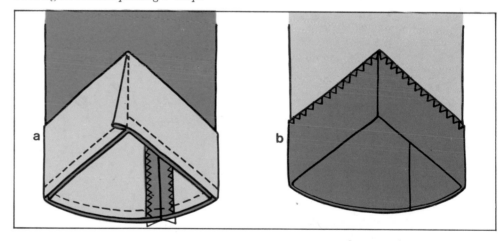

6 *Facing an inward pointing V-shape*

7 *Facing along a rever*

Collars

How often does a collar just not sit right on a garment and thus spoil the look? The difficulty often lies in getting the two curved edges eased in together but, with a little care, the collar can be set in perfectly to make it the additional fashion touch it should be. The main point to remember is to mark the shape very carefully and to make sure that both sides are exactly equal when you sew them. Topstitching the collar, close to the outer edge, is a good way of keeping a collar in shape and is not just meant as a decorative touch.

Collar groups

Most collars fall into one of three types: the first group encompasses flat collars, which turn away from the neckline and lie flat on the shoulder; an example is the Peter Pan collar. This type of collar has the neckline cut to the same shape as the neckline of the garment itself and it is the shape of the outer curve that enables the collar to lie flat. These collars, which are shaped at the neckline, should be cut with the straight of grain parallel to the centre back.

The second type includes turn-over or straight collars like shirt collars and collars with revers. These stand up at the back for about half their depth and then fold over. The neck edge of these collars is only very slightly curved and it is this joining of a straightish edge to a curved one, as well as the relation of the outer edge to the neck edge that causes the collar to rise and fall at the back neck edge.

The last category includes stand-up collars like mandarin collars and roll collars. These and straight, turn-over collars should be cut either exactly on the bias or exactly on the straight of the grain.

Cutting and facing

When cutting out collar patterns, make sure that if any alterations have been made to the neckline of the bodice, either these alterations do not affect the collar or that they are adapted to the collar as well. Sometimes, however, if you are altering shoulder seam lines, you will just need to recut the neckline of the bodice and not the collar.

If you are stiffening the collar on lightweight fabrics with an interfacing that is not an iron-on one, face the top collar and not the undercollar, so that all seam allowances will come under the interfacing. However, when working with an iron-on interfacing, face the undercollar, never the top collar. Interfacings may be taken into the seam and should, in these cases, be cut to the same size as the collar. When you are working with a heavy fabric they may, however, be cut exactly to the stitching line and be sewn to it with catchstitching. Unless working with a non-woven interfacing, cut the interfacing on exactly the same grain as the undercollar and tack it into position to the wrong side of the undercollar. With some styles, the undercollar is cut slightly smaller than the top collar.

Setting in

It is most important when setting in a collar to have the pattern pieces exactly matching at the centre back neck of both the collar and the bodice and for the front edges to be identical in shape and size and to meet exactly in the centre front. As the stitching lines of both edges are curved, they can tend to be stretched out of shape a little, depending on the fabric. This can be avoided by sewing a line of stay-stitching around these edges — or even just the neckline of the bodice — before they are sewn together. It is, in certain cases, a lot more successful to sew in a collar by hand — a greater degree of accuracy with the setting in is achieved this way. Where the collar is to be made up before attaching it to the garment, place the undercollar and top collar, right sides together, with the interfacing usually on the top collar and tack round the outer edges. Machine stitch from the undercollar side. Press the machine stitching then trim the seam allowance of the undercollar down to 0.2 cm ($\frac{1}{16}$in), the interfacing down to 0.3cm ($\frac{1}{8}$in) and the collar turning to 0.6cm ($\frac{1}{4}$in). This lessens the bulk in the edge of the collar and also avoids a ridge as the widest of the seam allowances will be against the top collar. Then clip all round the seam allowance at curves at 1.3cm ($\frac{1}{2}$in) intervals, cutting the corner of the seam allowance off diagonally in the case of pointed collars. Turn the collar to the right side and roll the edges, points and curves until the stitching line is just visible. Pull the seam very slightly to the underside of the collar and tack close to the edge with small stitches. Press the collar.

Flat collars: with a collar like a Peter Pan collar, tack and stitch top and undercollars together around outside edge, right sides together (Fig. 1a). This can be sewn on the machine but hand-sewing gives a more flexible stitching line and results in a better finish.

When there is no interfacing, trim the seam allowance of the undercollar to 0.6cm ($\frac{1}{4}$in) and that of the top collar to 1cm ($\frac{3}{8}$in). The thickness of the seam allowance is therefore graduated and prevents a ridge showing through when the two raw edges lie together inside the collar. If necessary, snip V-shaped notches out of the seam allowance all round the outer curve at 1.3cm ($\frac{1}{2}$in) intervals to reduce bulk and make the collar lie flat. Never do this on fine fabrics, however, as an ugly effect will be seen after pressing. Turn the collar to the right side and tack around the edge and across the width to keep it flat and in shape while sewing it in (Fig. 1b and c).

It is best not to press while the tackings are in as ridges will be made which are very difficult to remove again.

Turn-over collars: on a collar with a rever, the point of a knitting needle can be used to push out the corners when turning through to the right side. If you are using an interfacing, stiffen the undercollar and pin this interfaced

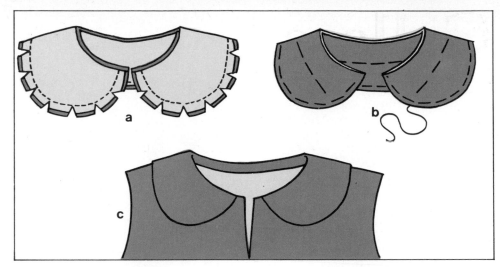

1 *Flat collar*

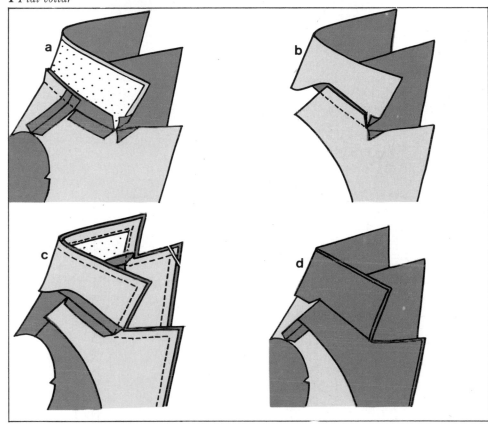

2 *Turn-over collar*

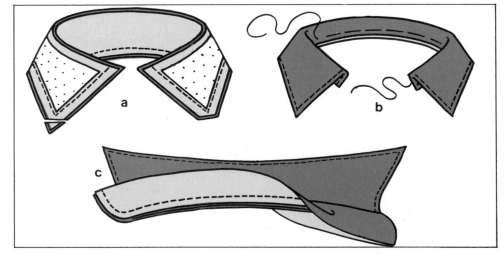

3 a, b, c *Making up a shirt collar*

25

undercollar only to the bodice neckline, matching the collar to garment at the centre back and centre front (Fig. 2a). Make sure that the revers are equal. Tack and machine the collar to the neckline as far as the stitching line at the ends. Snip the seam allowance and press it up into the collar at the back neck edge only and open from the shoulder seam to the front. Tack the facings to the top collar only, sew the front facing to the collar and then sew the collar pieces together all round. Turn to right side and tack just below the seam and press. Finish the back of the neck by turning the collar seam allowance under and slip-stitching it to the first line of stitching, or by bringing up the lining (if the garment is lined) over the edge of the collar (Fig. 2b and c).

Shirt collars: these are collars with a stand which usually fasten with a button and buttonhole at the centre front. Some have a separate band as well. The lower edge of the collar itself and the top edge of the band are equal in length but curved away from each other.

If the collar is to be worn open, face the undercollar; if the collar is to be done up at the neck, face the top collar instead. Place the top (more usually interfaced) and undercollar pieces together, right sides facing. Pin, tack and stitch along the front edges and the upper, curved seam. Trim the seam allowance to 0.6cm ($\frac{1}{4}$in), trim across the corners and turn to the right side (Fig 3a). Tack along the stitched edges and press.

If you are going to topstitch the collar, this is when to do it. Roll the collar into the position you would wear it and tack it firmly in this position along the seam line of the undercollar (Fig. 3b). Stitch the collar to the band; matching all markings, place the collar between the interfaced inner and outer collar band pieces, right sides facing, and stitch, leaving the lower edge open (Fig 3c). Trim the seam allowance to 0.6cm ($\frac{1}{4}$in) and turn to the right side. The ends of the collar band have now become tabs for the button and the buttonhole; if the tabs are too bulky, notch the seam allowance.

To attach the collar to the shirt, tack the front facing to the shirt along the neckline and pin the faced collar band along the inside of the neckline with raw edges level. Tack and sew (Fig. 3d). Trim the interfacing and the seam allowance of the band and press it into the collar; then turn under the seam allowance on the other collar band facing. Lay it over the stitching line to cover the machine

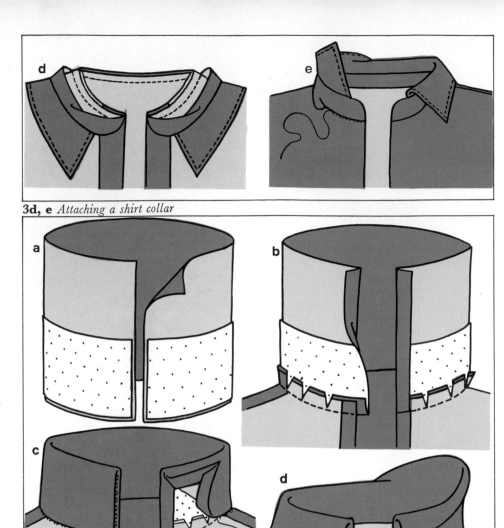

3d, e *Attaching a shirt collar*

4 *Stand-up collar*

5 *Mandarin collar*

6 *Detachable collars*

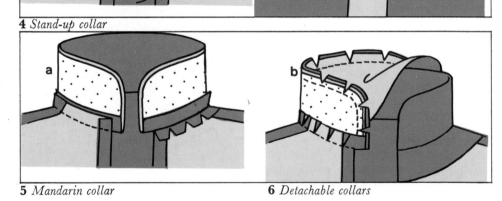

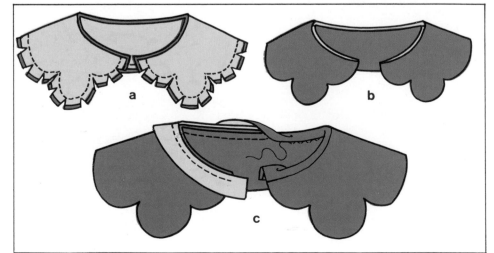

stitches and slipstitch neatly. Take care when hand-sewing the tab because this is the part that will be seen when the collar is buttoned (Fig. 3e).

Stand-up collars: with a roll collar, interface the underneath half of the collar only, if necessary, with a soft interfacing (Fig. 4a). Matching the centre back and centre front of the collar and garment, pin the collar, right sides together, at the interfaced edge. Tack and sew only as far as the ends of the stitching line. Trim and clip the seam allowance and press it upwards into the collar (Fig. 4b).
Turn in the ends of the collar and tack them down. Then turn in the raw edge of the top part of the collar and tack. Press. Bring the turned-in collar edge down on to the stitching line at the neck and, being careful to match the centre of the collar to the centre of the garment, pin, tack and slipstitch over the first row of stitches. Slipstitch the narrow ends of the collar to finish (Fig. 4c and d). With a stand-up collar like a mandarin collar, attach the interfaced outer collar piece to the neckline, right sides together, snip into the seam allowance and press it open (Fig. 5a). Tack the inner collar piece to the outer piece, with right sides together, and stitch carefully around the outside edges. Trim and snip this seam allowance, turn the collar to the right side so that the seam is on the top, tack and press. Finish off the lower edge as for a shirt collar and cover this edge with a facing. If there is a zip fastener to be inserted in the bodice, put this in before attaching the collar (Fig. 5b).

Detachable collars: these are a clever idea for varying the appearance of a plain dress or blouse and, if you make up a number in a variety of thin fabrics used to make blouses, they can be attached to suit jackets too for matching effect.
Make the collars to the size and shape required, leaving the neck edge unfinished (Fig. 6a). Cut a bias strip of fabric 3cm (1¼in) wide and 5cm (2in) longer than the neckline of the collar. Tack the strip around the neck edge of the collar, leaving 2.5cm (1in) projecting at each end and tacking 0.3cm (⅛in) outside the stitching line, thus reducing the width of the neckline seam allowance by 0.3cm (⅛in). Stitch along the line of the tacking and trim the seam allowance at the neck edge to 0.6cm (¼in). Neaten the edges of the bias strip and press the binding to the underside of the collar so that, when attached to

the actual neckline of the garment, it fits exactly (Fig. 6b and c).

Above. *The classic styling of a revers collar suits any shirt.*

Darts

The object of a dart is to remove fullness and to shape a garment to fit the curves of the body. It is extremely important that all darts start and finish in exactly the right position for the individual figure.

Check the pattern against your figure by either testing the pattern in cotton or calico or by measuring the pattern piece from seamline to seamline and comparing it with your own measure-ments. Alter the pattern accordingly, before cutting out, remembering to take into account the body ease allowed in each pattern piece.

Adjustments to the bustline

The bust area should fit smoothly but enough ease must be allowed to ensure comfortable movement. The darts should point towards the fullest part of the bust (Fig. 1).

High or low bustlines: to check whether your bustline is higher or lower than the pattern, measure from the middle of the shoulder to the tip of the bust. On the pattern draw inter-secting lines through the bust darts to locate the bust point. Then compare the two measurements.

If the bust is high, the bodice fullness will fall below the bust, causing pulling across the actual bustline (Fig. 2a). If

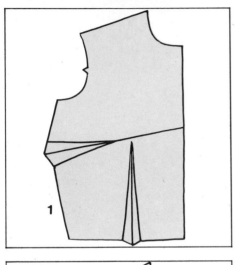

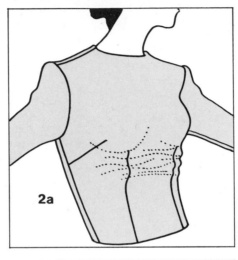

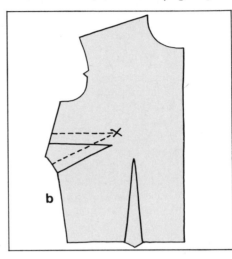

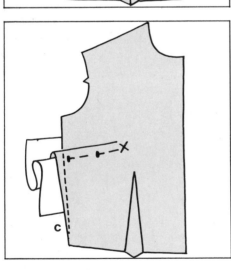

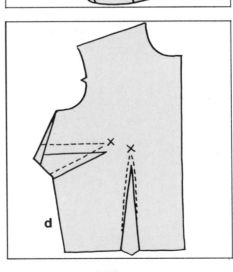

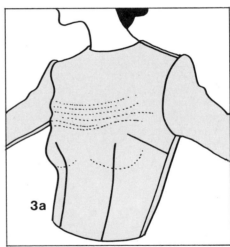

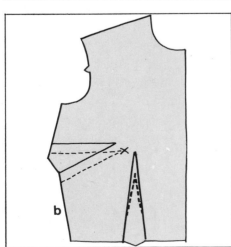

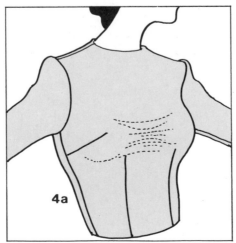

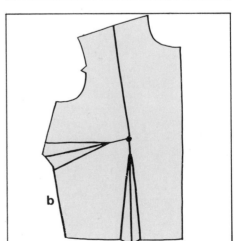

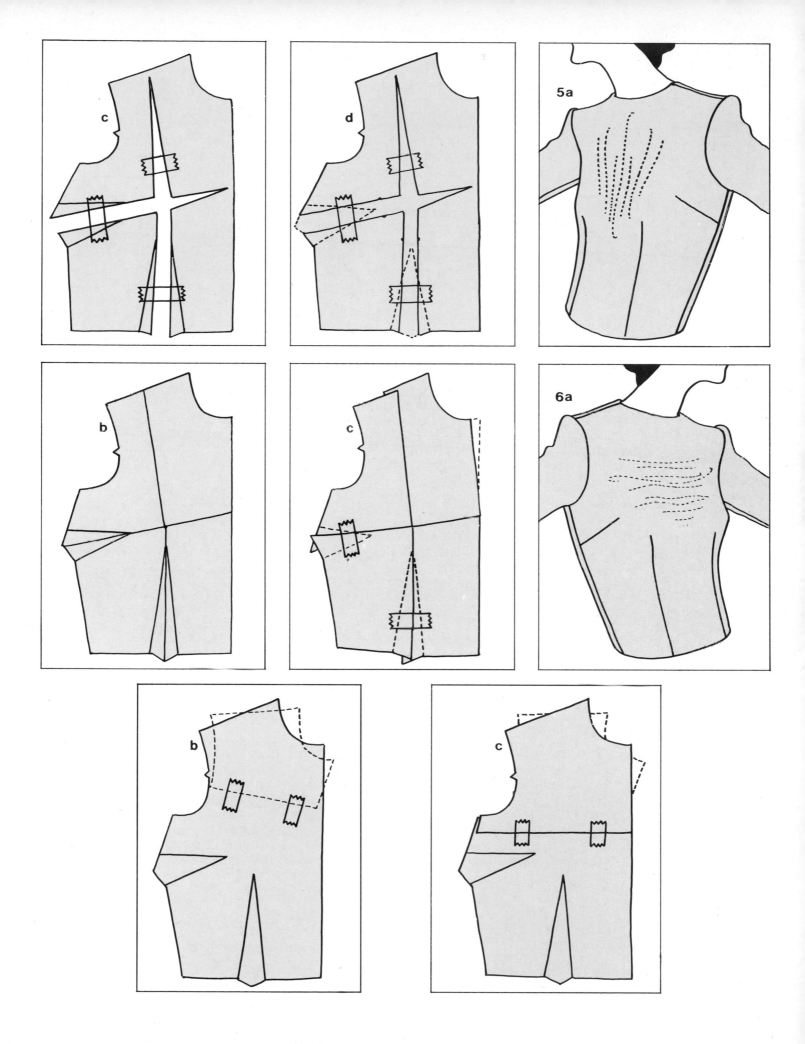

low, the fullness will fall above the bustline, causing a pulling across the bust (Fig. 3a).

To remedy, determine the amount of adjustment required, measure from the original dart point and mark (Fig. 2b). Raise or lower each of the dart lines by the same amount and mark them at the side seam. Redraw the dart lines in the correct position, parallel to the original. To obtain the correct shape at the side seam, tape a piece of tissue underneath the side seam edge, fold the new dart and pin it in place and out along the side cutting line (Fig. 2c). If the bodice has a waistline dart, an equal adjustment must be made with the point of the dart raised or lowered by the same amount as the bust dart and the lines adjusted to this point (Fig. 2d).

Large bust: this would cause pulling across the bust area (Fig. 4a). Draw a line through the centre of the underarm and through the waistline dart (Fig. 4b). The bustline is located at the intersection of these two lines. From this point, draw a line to the centre of the shoulder. Slash along the vertical line from the waistline to within 0.3in ($\frac{1}{8}$cm) of the shoulder seam. Slash on the horizontal line to within 0.3cm ($\frac{1}{8}$in) of the centre front line. Place the pattern on a sheet of tissue and spread it on the vertical slash at the bust point by half the amount required. Spread the pattern on the horizontal slash at the bust point by half the amount required. Tape in place (Fig. 4c). Mark the new dart positions in the centre of each slash and shorten each dart from this point by 2.5cm (1in) (Fig. 4d). Re-draw the darts from the new points to the original dart lines at the side seam and the waistline.

Smaller than average bust: folds of fabric will fall across the bust area (Fig. 5a).

To obtain less shaping the bust dart must be decreased. Draw a line through the centre of the underarm dart and the waistline dart (Fig. 5b). The bust point lies at the intersection of the two lines. Draw a line from the bust point to the centre of the shoulders. Slash along the vertical line from the waistline

within 0.3cm ($\frac{1}{8}$in) of the shoulder seam. Then slash along the horizontal line to within 0.3cm ($\frac{1}{8}$in) of the centre front. Overlap both the vertical and horizontal slashes at the bust point, each by half the required amount and tape in place. This decreases both darts. The new dart point should now be located where the dart stitching lines intersect. Re-draw the centre front line (Fig. 5c).

Hollow chest: causes too much fullness between the neckline and the bust. The distance from the neckline to the bust must be shortened on the pattern to eliminate the excess fullness (Fig. 6a). Determine the amount of adjustment to be made, trace the outline of the pattern at the centre front, neckline and shoulder and armhole on to tissue paper and draw a line square with the grain line from the underarm edge to the centre front. Leave this aside until required. Slash the bodice front horizontally from the centre front to the armhole seamline about 10cm (4in) below the neckline edge. Overlap the slash line at the centre front by the necessary amount and tape in place (Fig. 6c).

Place the tracing of the front pattern over the pattern piece to obtain a straight centre front line above the slash line. Tape in place. Use the traced neckline, shoulder and armhole to obtain the original shape and size of pattern.

Sewing and pressing darts

When sewing a dart, keep the fabric absolutely flat. Fold the dart so that the lines are exactly together and pin so that the fabric lies flat. Tack the dart, starting at the wide end, and leave the end of the thread free at the point. Remove tailor tacks and check the length by measuring along the fold of the fabric, then measure the corresponding dart on the other side of the garment. If the sides of the dart are straight, draw a chalk line on which to machine stitch. Press the fold so that the fabric lies flat and carefully machine the dart, starting from the outside edge, making the final stitches actually run off the fold at the point. Either sew in the ends of the thread by hand or use reverse stitch on the machine. If reverse

stitching, take care to reverse close to the fold or else the line of the dart will be spoilt.

Dart tucks: these are similar to darts but they are left as pleats. Work and handle as for darts and press either to one side or with an equal amount pressed to either side.

Double-pointed darts: these usually form a diamond shape and are usually made on a dress with no waist seam. Sew them in two sections, beginning at the centre and tapering the stitches off at each end as at the point of a single dart.

After pressing, snip the fold of the dart at the centre to prevent any pulling and then oversew the snip to prevent fraying.

Pressing

Pressing darts must be done carefully, vertical darts at waist and shoulder being pressed towards the centre of the garment and horizontal darts at bust or elbow being pressed downwards. Press the fabric on either side of the darts carefully, using the point of the iron along the stitching line. Then press the darts to one side.

When working on thick, heavy fabrics, it is a good idea to slash the dart to within about one inch of the point, in order to reduce bulk, and overcast the edges.

Press the dart open with a piece of card between the dart seam and the main fabric to avoid a ridge on the right side of the garment.

Where fullness results at the point of a dart, particularly on a heavy fabric, shrink it away.

To do this, take a length of fine, matching thread or silk and run a circle through the back threads of the fabric, large enough to enclose the fullness. Ensure that the stitches do not show through on the right side.

Draw up the silk a little and then place the garment, right side down on a pressing ham, cover with a wet piece of fabric (the same material if this is possible), lay a hot iron over it, then lift the iron quickly and allow the steam to escape.

Sleeves

Succeeding in making a sleeve sit correctly in the armhole of a garment is generally considered to be the most difficult part of dressmaking.

The bodice of the garment and the sleeves should be made up as far as possible before the sleeves are set into the armholes to avoid unnecessary creasing of the fabric. Firstly make sure that all notches are in place on the pattern and that those on the garment armholes and sleeves will match up. The sleeve crown should be 3-4cm (1-1½in) larger than the bodice armhole so that the sleeve may be eased into the armhole at the top to fit smoothly and comfortably over the rounded top of the arm.

Making up and setting in the sleeve

Tack the sleeve dart, if there is one. Then tack the underarm seam of the sleeve from the armhole to the wrist. There are two ways of easing the sleeve into the armhole. One is by working two rows of gathering stitches, one on the stitching line and one 0.6cm (¼in) outside, between the front and back notches. The surplus fabric is eased in on these threads so that the front and back and crown notches on the sleeve match up with those on the armhole (Fig. 1a and b).

The second way of easing in this sleeve fullness is where the armhole and crown seam allowances are held, with the raw edges towards you and with the sleeve edge uppermost. The surplus fabric of the crown is eased into the armhole, inserting pins vertically at about 1.3cm (½in) intervals (Fig. 2a and b).

Pin the sleeve to the sleeve head of the garment being worn and ease in the fullness either by pulling up the gathering stitches or by pinning to the armhole of the garment. The sleeve crown point must be matched to the shoulder seam. The grain of the fabric should hang straight and there should not be any wrinkling of the sleeve. It is best to work with both sleeves at the same time so that both sleeves will be identical in shape on completion. If the sleeve does not hang correctly, repitch the sleeve more to the front or to the back of the garment until it looks right. If an alteration has been necessary, mark the new sleeve crown point to match the shoulder seam (Fig. 3a and b).

With the sleeve and the bodice right side out, place the underarm seam of the sleeve to the underarm seam of the bodice. If there is no seam match the notches. Work on the sleeve through the armhole and not from bodice of the garment. Pin and tack the sleeve to the armhole at the seam and for about 8cm (3in) to either side of the seam. Take care not to stretch the sleeve at this point because the whole section is on the cross. Pin and tack the other sleeve in the same way. Stitch in sleeves and press the seams towards the blouse. Trim the seam allowance and flat fell the seams. Press over the end of a sleeve board. Use double thread and backstitch by hand for a good finish or, carefully, machine stitch round the armhole. For additional strength, machine stitch over a row of backstitching. Do not snip or trim the seam allowances but press them towards the sleeve.

With woollen and cotton fabrics, excess ease may be shrunk away after pinning by holding a warm iron over a damp cloth over the sleeve head.

Loose-lined long sleeves

For loose-lined long sleeves, make up and press the sleeves. Make up the linings in the same way but a little larger than the sleeves themselves, simply by taking a slightly smaller seam allowance. Press the seam allowances open. With the sleeve wrong side out and the lining with the right side out, slip the lining on to the sleeve. Match up the seams and the darts and work a row of tacking stitches along the seams, leaving a few inches free at top and bottom (Fig. 4a). Continue working rows of tacking all round the sleeve to keep the lining and sleeve together. Turn up the hem on each sleeve and catchstitch (Fig. 4b). Turn up the lining so that the hem is about 1.3cm (½in) higher than the lower edge of the sleeve and slipstitch (Fig. 4c). Press each sleeve, then set it in.

Lined sleeves are finished by tacking the bodice lining to the seam allowance of the sleeve. Turn under the seam allowance on the crown of the sleeve lining to the wrong side and tack (Fig. 5a). Matching underarm seams and notches, pin the fold edge of the sleeve to just over the tacking stitches. Tack and slipstitch into position. Because of

Right. *A batwing sleeve — cut out as one with the bodice sewn with a single seam.*

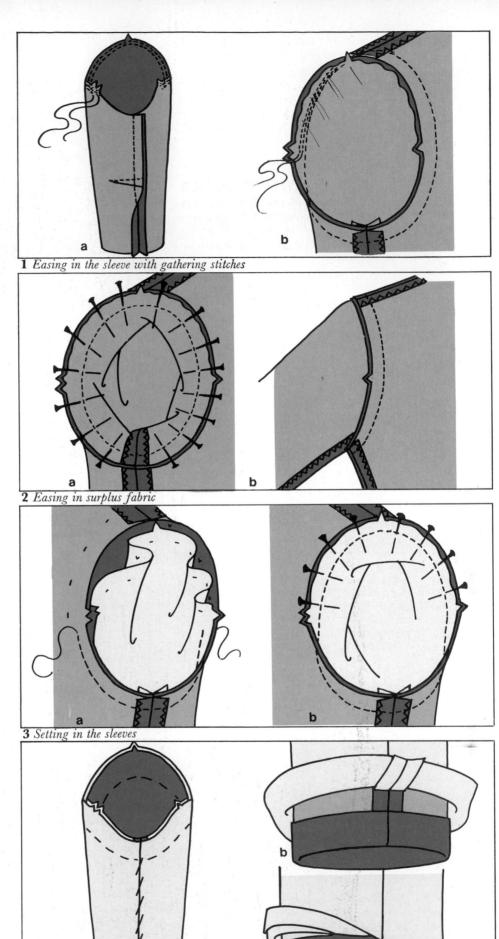

1 *Easing in the sleeve with gathering stitches*

2 *Easing in surplus fabric*

3 *Setting in the sleeves*

4 *Loose-lined long sleeve*

the nature of lining fabrics it will not be possible to ease away fullness but when setting in the actual sleeves make tiny tucks over the sleeve head (Fig. 5b).

Sleeves without cuffs: If sleeves are not to be set into a cuff, the edges should be finished in one of the following ways.

Short sleeves should end with a hem or a facing. The lower edge of a short sleeve is sometimes inclined to lift at the side of the sleeve so rectify this before finishing off the hem. Try it on and trim the line if necessary. Tack the hem and slipstitch it into position. It is best to handstitch, and not use the machine for sleeve hems but topstitching is a good idea for firm fabrics to give a good finish. If the edge is faced, use a bias strip of fabric or binding which sits flat against the slightly shaped seam line. Pin the right side of the strip to the right side of the sleeve, so that the join will come over the sleeve seam. Tack and machine stitch the facing in place, then fold it to the wrong side of the sleeve and slipstitch it in place (Fig. 6a and b).

Long fitted sleeves need an opening (Fig. 7a). Leave the sleeve seam open for 6 to 8cm (2½ to 3in) above the wrist stitching line so that the sleeve will pass easily over the hand. Stitch the continuation of the side of the seam allowance nearest the back of the sleeve down to form a hem, first turning it in narrowly to neaten. Snip across the other side of the seam allowance at the base of the seam to free the width of the seam allowance and sew a bias strip to it. Any raw edges left at the top of the opening must be neatened and reinforced with loop stitch (Fig. 7b and c).

Neaten the lower edge of the sleeve to suit the thickness of the fabric—either by turning up an ordinary narrow hem, hem, by making a narrow facing of the garment fabric or by binding with bias binding, mitring at the corner to neaten.

Sew press fasteners or hooks and eyes to close the opening and sew a bar tack at the top of the opening to strengthen it. On a long sleeve of very thin fabric, just roll up the hem and slipstitch, rolling up about 7.5cm (3in) along the inner wrist slightly more. This will eliminate the necessity for an opening.

Raglan sleeves

This sleeve is joined to both back and front bodice pieces by a seam that runs from the underarm slanting up to the neckline edge. With right sides together, matching notches, tack and stitch the sleeve to the back and front bodice sections using a flat fell seam (Fig. 8a and b).

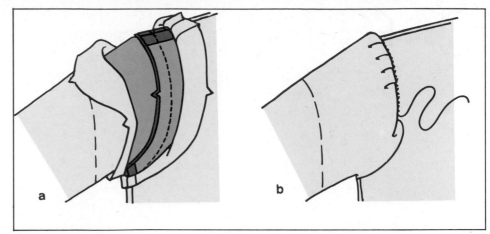

5 *Finishing lined sleeves*

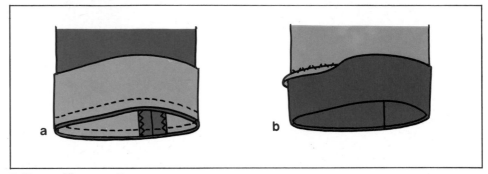

6 *Sleeve without a cuff*

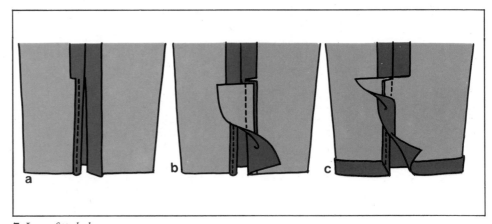

7 *Long fitted sleeve*

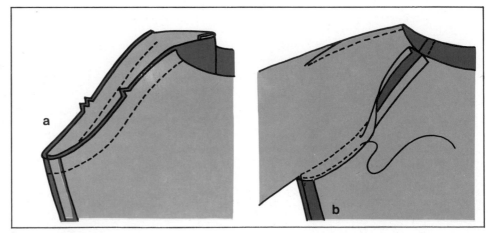

8 *Raglan sleeve*

Cuffs

There are three basic methods of finishing off a sleeve with a cuff. The turn-back cuff, the straight band and the shirt-style band. All cuffs are made from double fabric with a layer of interfacing in between. Iron-on interfacing is suitable for the small area involved in a cuff.

Turn-back cuffs are cut all in one with the sleeve and are usually set on long sleeves on heavier fabrics. The sleeve side seam may be curved to allow the cuff to lie flat against the sleeve. Attach the interfacing before sewing up the sleeve seam, then sew the whole seam, including the cuff. Press the seam open, snipping the seam allowance in the cuff section (Fig. 1a and b).
Turn under the lower edge to the wrong side, tack and press. Neaten the raw edge by overcasting by hand or machine and stitch to the sleeve with invisible hemming stitch (Fig. 1c and d). Fold the cuff back into position and work a bar tack near the sleeve side seam between the cuff and the sleeve.

Straight bands are sewn separately and can be made up in a contrast to pick up a colour in another garment, such as the blouse fabric for the band on a jacket sleeve. For each sleeve cut a band and band facing, either on the same grain as the sleeve or on the bias. Interface the bands. Join the seams of the bands and of the band facing. With right sides together, matching the seam to the underarm seam, tack and stitch the band to the lower sleeve edge. Grade the seam allowance and press it open (Fig. 2a and b).
Join the inner, unfaced, band to the lower edge of the outer band. Grade the seam allowance and press the seam open. Fold the band facing to the inside and tuck around the fold edge. Press the edge flat. Tack the lower edge and finish with herringbone stitch. Press flat. If the sleeve is being lined, draw the lining down over the join of sleeve and cuff and hem in position (Fig. 2c and d).

Shirt cuffs are made from one, folded piece of fabric if they are straight or from two pieces with a seam around the outer edges if shaped. Interface one section of the cuff and mark the button-hole positions. Make the sleeve opening as described in the chapter on sleeves

Right. *The smart turn-back cuff highlighted by the use of decorative buttons.*

and work a double row of gathering stitches around the lower edge of the sleeve (Fig. 3a).

With the right sides together, pin the ends of the cuff to the sleeve. Arrange the gathers evenly to fit the cuff with little gathering either side of the sleeve seam and most of the fullness at the ends. Pin, tack and stitch the cuff to the sleeve (Fig. 3b and c).

A neater sleeve line is achieved if the buttonhole edge is set level with the sleeve opening, with the surplus cuff fabric and the button as an underlap. Neaten the seam inside.

Open cuffs are usually made on lighter fabrics and set on short sleeves. These cuffs can be straight or shaped with the seam sloping towards the lower edge of the cuff. Open cuffs are turned back from the sleeve and are made from two pieces of fabric with an interfacing set to the inner pieces. With right sides together, pin, tack and stitch the cuff facing to the cuff along the outer edge and ends. Grade the seam allowance and snip off corners to give a good line (Fig. 4a).

Turn the cuff to the right side and tack around the stitched edge and press flat. Set it on to the sleeve. With right sides together and with seams and raw edges level, tack and stitch the cuff to the sleeve through all layers of fabric. Press the seam allowance up towards the sleeve. Neaten the raw edge. On the right side work a row of stitching close to the cuff seam line to hold the seam allowance in place. A bar tack can be worked at the top corner of the cuffs to hold them in place (Fig. 4b and c). On a lighter fabrics the corners can be caught together with a stitch or two.

Gauntlet cuffs are similar in appearance to turn-back cuffs but they are not cut all in one with the sleeve. They are usually made on long sleeves on coats and jackets. Cut two pieces of fabric for each cuff and interface one of them to be the undercuff. (fig. 5a)

Stitch the two pieces together along the top edge, then stitch the cuff at the side seam. Place the cuff to the sleeve, with right sides together, raw edges level, matching side seams, and tack all round lower edge. Stitch all round and trim the seam allowance narrowly. Turn down the top cuff and tack all round the sleeve through all layers of fabric just above the hem line to hold the cuff in position. Turn the sleeve to the wrong side, fold the top cuff to the wrong side and, turning in the raw edge narrowly, stitch it to the inside of the sleeve (Fig. 5b and c).

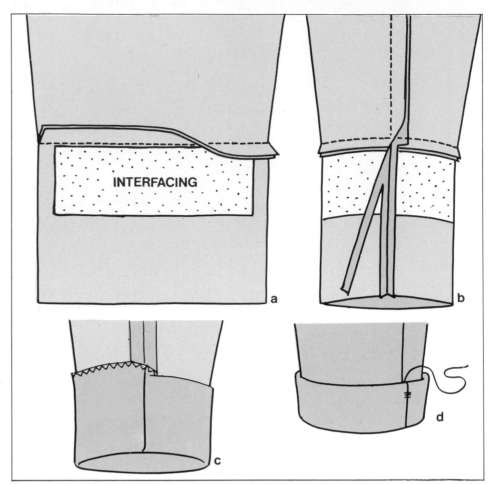

1 *Turn-back cuffs*

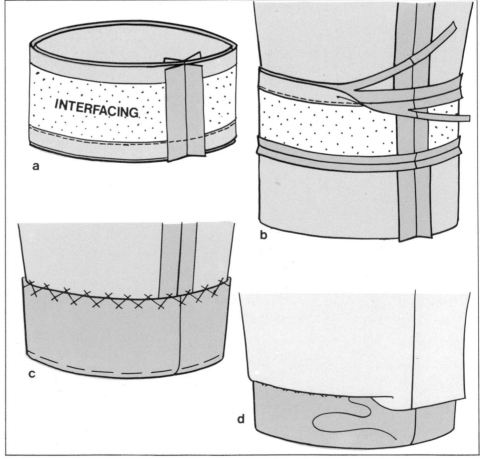

2 *Straight band cuffs*

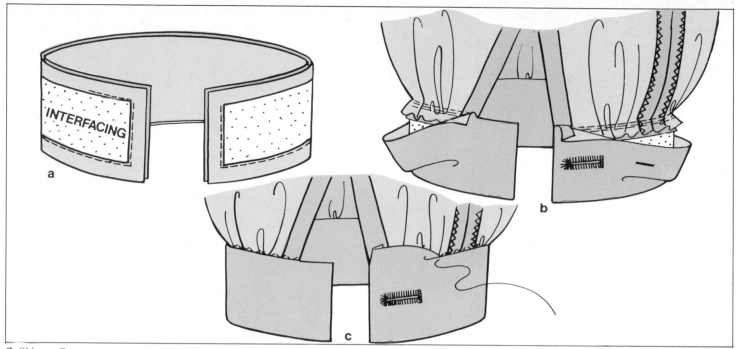

3 *Shirt cuffs*

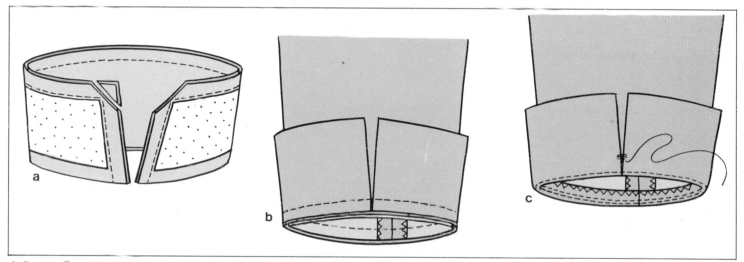

4 *Open cuffs*

5 *Gauntlet cuffs*

Buttons

If purchasing buttons choose then at the same time as the fabric to ensure correct colour and style matching. For example, choose plain buttons for a classic tweed country coat, leather for a car coat, silver or gilt for a blazer. There is a wide selection of decorative buttons from which to make a choice for dresses and blouses but make sure that the buttons chosen are not too heavy for the style and fabric of the garment, and that they are washable if they are to go on a washable fabric.

Making self-fabric covered buttons

A fabric-covered button should only be used with a bound buttonhole as the friction of a hand-worked buttonhole will soon wear away the fabric covering the button. Do not use stiff, shiny fabric for making a covered button as it is very difficult to mould around the button. If using a loosely woven fabric line it first. There are special button mounts which are simple to cover but old buttons can be used from the button box. They can be odd ones provided they are the same shape on the underside.

Cut a circle of fabric a little larger than the button, using double thread work a row of small running stitches all round, close to the edge. Place the button in the centre of the fabric and pull the thread to draw up the fullness (Fig. 1a and b). Fasten off the thread firmly. Cut a smaller circle of fabric to just cover the stitching, turn in the raw edge and sew to cover the line of stitching on the underside of the button. Sew the button to the garment through the original holes with strong thread (Fig. 1c).

Sewing on a button with a self-shank

Buttons must always be sewn on to double fabric. If the fabric is single, it must be reinforced with a scrap of fabric, tape or ribbon. This reinforcement can be either hemmed to the back of the fabric or simply held in place by the button stitching. In either case, the edges of the reinforcement should be neatened. Buttons should be sewn on before any loops are made but after buttonholes have been worked (Fig. 2). Commence by making a small back-stitch in the fabric, then thread the button on to the thread and sew. With

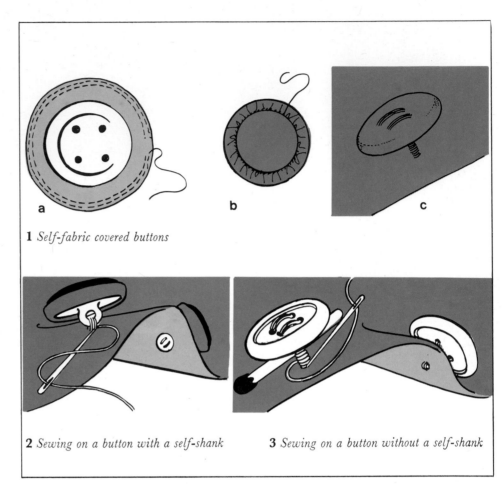

1 *Self-fabric covered buttons*

2 *Sewing on a button with a self-shank*

3 *Sewing on a button without a self-shank*

six or eight stitches through the shank, form a bar on the wrong side. Where the button is heavy or the fabric thick, a stay (or keeper) button should always be sewn at the back of the fabric just behind the top button to strengthen it. The stay button should be small, round and flat and should have the same number of holes as the top button and should be sewn on at the same time as the shanked button.

Sewing on a button without a self-shank

If the button has two or four holes instead of having a moulded shank, a shank of strong thread must be made for it. This ensures that the fabric underneath the button is not puckered by it; the thicker the fabric, the longer the shank must be made. With two-holed buttons, arrange the holes to run parallel with the buttonhole. Sew through the holes six or eight times starting in the same way as before, taking care to sew through the same positions each time, so that a neat bar of stitches is

formed on the wrong side. After the first stitch has been taken through the button, insert two or three pins between the fabric and the button to lengthen the stitches and to give depth for the shank. If the fabric is very thick, use matchsticks instead of pins. When the stitching is finished, pass the needle through the button but not the fabric and remove the pins. Wind the thread firmly around the "stem" between the button and the fabric to form the shank and then take the needle through to the back of the fabric to finish off. Work loop stitch over the bar of stitches formed at the back of the fabric and fasten off with a back stitch (Fig. 3).

With four-holed buttons, work in the same way but sew either to make two bars or a cross. If making two bars, arrange for the needle to come out at only two points at the back to end up with a bar in the same way as for a two-holed button. If making a cross, work each diagonal alternatively.

Buttonholes

Buttonholes are made on the right-hand side of the opening for women's clothing, on the left for men's and, depending on the type of garment, can be worked by hand or machine.

The position of the buttonhole is usually marked on the paper pattern but, if alterations have been made, re-measure and re-mark. If a row of buttonholes is to be made, the distance between them must be measured carefully with a ruler and the positions marked with tailor's chalk or pins. The buttonhole should be no closer to the edge of the garment than the diameter of the button so that, when fastened, the button does not extend over the edge of the garment.

Hand-worked buttonholes

Buttonholes are always worked on double fabric so ensure that the facing or turning goes back far enough. And, it is best to have an interfacing of some sort to give a strong base for the button-holes. Allow 45cm (18in) thread for working a 1.3cm ($\frac{1}{2}$in) long buttonhole, 68cm (29in) thread for a 2.5cm (1in) buttonhole and so on. This avoids making a join in the thread, which spoils the line of the buttonhole.

Buttonholes are worked vertically on blouse or dress fronts that have front panels or bands, and horizontally on cuffs, belts, waistbands and on plain dress and blouse fronts. This is because the direction of the buttonhole must follow the line of the strain.

Horizontally worked buttonholes are shaped round at one end and straight at the other. The round end is to accommodate the shank of the button and the straight end is to keep the buttonhole in shape. Vertical buttonholes are made with two straight ends. Buttonholes are therefore never made with two round ends. Always work on a test piece first. Tack around each marked buttonhole to hold all layers of fabric together. Cut the first buttonhole, starting with the one that will show the least. By the time a couple have been worked, the tension will have improved. Using sharp, pointed scissors or special buttonhole scissors, cut the buttonhole to the diameter of the button plus 0.3cm ($\frac{1}{8}$in).

Begin at the end furthest away from the edge of the garment (or at the bottom on vertical buttonholes) and work the stitch from left to right. Either oversew the raw edges first or lay a strand of thread along the edge of the slit and work the buttonhole stitch over it. Use

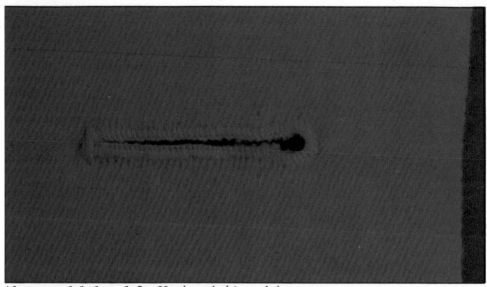

Above and below left. *Hand worked buttonholes.*

Below right. *Piped buttonholes worked on thicker fabrics.*

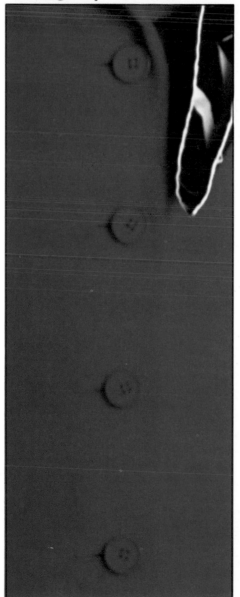

your thumb-nail as a guide to regulate the depth. Bring the needle out at the right-hand end of the slit. Carry the thread upward and to the left, then down and to the right, forming a loop, which should be held down with the thumb. Insert the needle under the cut edge and bring it out just below the strand and over the loop. Pull up the needle sharply so that a knot is formed on the edge of the slit (Fig. 1a). Repeat this stitch to the end of the first side, then work five or seven stitches round in a fan shape then continue along the other side of the slit to the starting point. Then work two strands of thread straight across the end to form a bar and work over them in loop stitch, keeping the knotted edge towards the buttonhole and the stitches free from the fabric (Fig. 1b).

Machine-made buttonholes

If the length of the buttonhole can be set automatically, mark only the start of the buttonhole with chalk. Do not use tacking stitches, as these are difficult to remove later. Fasten off thread ends and cut the buttonholes carefully.

Bound buttonholes

Bound buttonholes are started before the facing is put on and finished after, so tack a strip of interfacing to the back of the fabric before working. Then, when the facing has been attached to the garment, make slits in the facing to correspond with the buttonholes, turn in the edges of these slits and slipstitch in place round the buttonhole.

After marking the position of the buttonhole, cut a piece of fabric 8cm (3in) deep and 5cm (2in) wider than the length required for the buttonhole. Mark the line for the buttonhole exactly in the centre of this piece of fabric. Place it, right side on to the right side of the garment, with the buttonhole markings matching (Fig. 2a). Tack the two

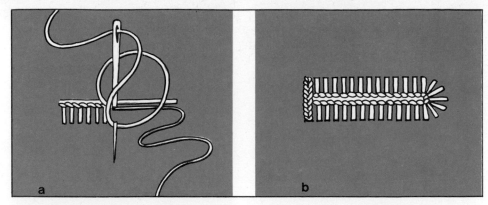

1 *Sewing hand-worked buttonholes*

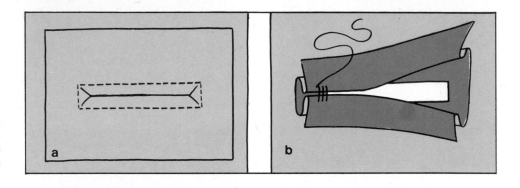

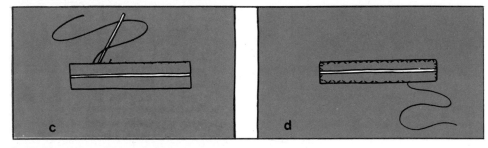

2 *Making a bound buttonhole*

pieces together then machine 0.3cm ($\frac{1}{8}$in) from the marking all round it. Cut along the line with scissors and, at each end, cut diagonally into each corner, stopping just short of the stitching. Turn the piece of fabric through to the back of the garment, press the small

seams open and then fold so that the edges meet and form an inverted pleat at each end (Fig. 2b and c). Slipstitch the edges at the back.

From the right side of the garment, prickstitch in place along the buttonhole stitching line (Fig. 2d).

Zip fasteners

There are zips designed to meet every dressmaking and tailoring need, and some thought should be given to this variety before purchasing one. There is also the choice between metal and nylon zip teeth, both being equally good in the correct application, although care must be taken not to damage the nylon teeth when ironing.

The zip

A zip consists of two rows of interlocking teeth secured to two strips of tape, to which the garment fabric is sewn. The two strips of tape are secured with an end stop and the teeth are opened or closed by the slider. The slider and end stop take up about 1.3cm ($\frac{1}{2}$in) of the effective zip length (Fig. 1a and b).

Length of zip required

Before purchasing the zip for a particular garment, consult the pattern envelope for the suggested length and always purchase this length unless the pattern is to be shortened or lengthened. If in doubt, leave the purchase of the zip until the garment is fitted.

Do not purchase too short a zip as this causes strain and the zip might break, thus needing replacement.

The opening left in a garment for inserting a zip should always be a little longer than the actual zip teeth to allow the fabric to be eased slightly to the tape. Allow 0.16cm ($\frac{1}{16}$in) extra opening per 2.5cm (1in) of zip i.e. 20cm (8in) zip = 21.5cm (8$\frac{1}{2}$in) opening. For zips longer than 40cm (16in), allow 2.5cm (1in) extra.

Also, the zip teeth should never go right up to the neck finish or waist band, so allow an extra 0.6cm ($\frac{1}{4}$in) here (Fig. 2a).

Zip seams

When machining the zip seam, finish the end off very securely. This prevents strain on the zip (Fig. 2b).

Semi-concealed zips

This method is used on dresses with collars, either at the front or the back, medium to thick weight tweed skirts, trousers and open ended zips.

Preparation of dress for long zip.

Snip through the waist seam 3.2cm (1$\frac{1}{4}$in) from the edge of the opening and

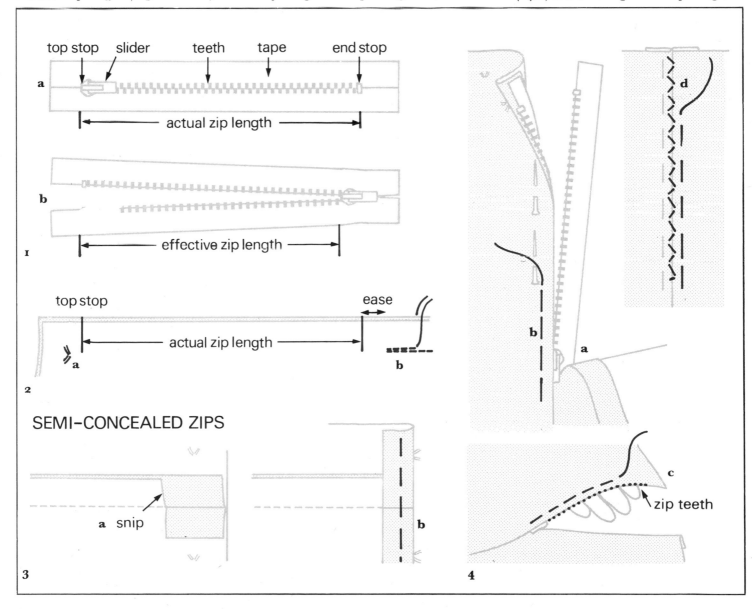

press firmly open (Fig. 3a).

Tack and press the zip opening back on the seam line (Fig. 3b). Open the zip and place it behind the folded edges of the opening with the end stop to the end of the machining (Fig. 4a).

Pin and tack one side of the zip in place, with the zip teeth just behind the fold and tacking 0.6cm (¼in) from the fold (Fig. 4b). The extra length allowed for the opening is eased along the zip length by holding the zip and fabric as shown (Fig. 4c).

Bring up the other side of the zip and catch the two fold edges together (Fig. 4d), so that the two sides can be matched in length and pattern.

Tack the second side 0.6cm (¼in) away from the fold.

For a couture finish, sew in the zip by hand using a tiny half back stitch, Work each side from the bottom up, angling the bottom end to the seam line (Fig. 5). If you wish to machine the zip in place, use a zipper foot to allow the stitching to be closer to the zip.

Machine to within 5cm (2in) of the top of the zip, leave the needle in the work and lift the foot (Fig. 6a).

Unpick 7.5cm (3in) of the catch tacking and ease the zip slider down past the foot (Fig. 6b). Complete the machining. This method prevents the stitching line from widening at the slider.

Neaten the back by stitching the zip to the seam allowance (Fig. 7).

Decorative zips

These are used in pinafore dresses and pockets.

Tack the zip in place as shown for the semi-concealed zips. Sew the facings in place and complete the hem.

For a pinafore dress, top stitch round the neck and down the hem, 0.6cm (¼in) away from all edges (Fig. 8).

For pockets, top stitch evenly all round the zip before applying the pocket bag to the garment.

Open ended zips

Assemble the garment, leaving the zip opening between the facings and the fronts. Press the turnings back (Fig. 9a). Separate the zip and slip the sections in the openings, and place so that the teeth are just hidden behind the fold (Fig. 9b). Pin and tack through the front, the zip tape and the facing (Fig. 9c). Top stitch, using strong thread or buttonhole twist threaded on top of the machine (Fig. 9d).

Concealed zips

These are used on dresses without collars, lightweight fabric skirts and

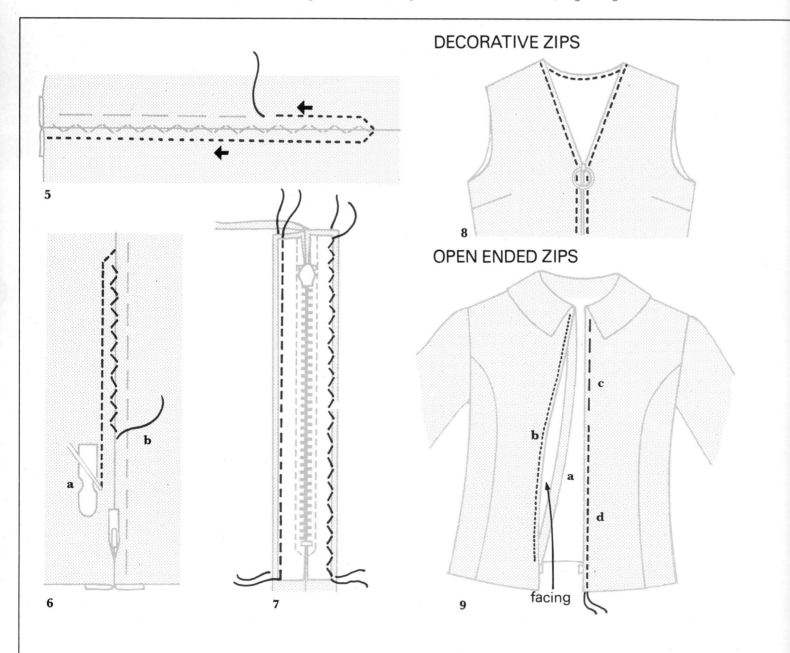

DECORATIVE ZIPS

OPEN ENDED ZIPS

5

6

7

8

9

facing

trousers.

Note: The zip seam should be cut with a 2.5cm (1in) allowance.

Preparation of dress facing.

Place the right side of the neck facing to the right side of the dress, matching shoulder seams and centre front. On the left hand side, turn back the facing 0.6cm (¼in) from the dress sewing line. Turn the dress seam allowance back to the sewing line (Fig. 10a). On the right hand side, take the facing straight to the edge (Fig. 10b).

Machine the facing in place, and trim the seam to 0.6cm (¼in). Snip at 1.3cm (½in) intervals (Fig. 10c). Hand stitch the facing to the seam (Fig. 10d).

Turn the seam allowance of the left hand side of the dress to the wrong side and press flat (Fig. 10c).

For all openings using this concealed zip method, work a line of catch tacks along the sewing lines of the opening (Fig. 10f).

For side skirt or trouser zip, read 'back' for 'right hand side' and 'front' for 'left hand side'.

Snip the right hand side seam allowance to within 0.3cm (⅛in) of the seam, 1.3cm (½in) below the end of the opening (Fig. 11a).

Fold the turning along this new line so that the seam allowance projects beyond the seam line by 0.3cm (⅛in) (Fig. 11b).

Place the zip right side uppermost behind this line, with the end stop in line with the end of the opening. Pin and tack in place, with the fold just missing the zip teeth (Fig. 11c).

Hem firmly right down to the end of the 0.3cm (⅛in) extension (Fig. 11d).

Snip the remaining 0.3cm (⅛in) seam allowance (Fig. 11e).

Bring the left hand side over so that the fold lies along the original sewing line on the right hand side. Catch tack in place (Fig. 11f). Tack 1.3cm (½in) away from the fold on the left hand side (Fig. 11g).

Using a half back stitch, sew up from the seam line at an angle and up the 1.3cm (½in) line, or machine taking care to stitch a straight line (Fig. 11h). Fig. 11i illustrates the wrong side of the garment and zip, showing how it should lie in place.

Zip guards

These are used to protect underwear and sensitive skins from being rubbed by the zip teeth, and they give a very professional finish to the garment. Measure the zip opening and add 3.8 cm (1½in). Cut one piece of lining and one piece of fabric (Fig. 12).

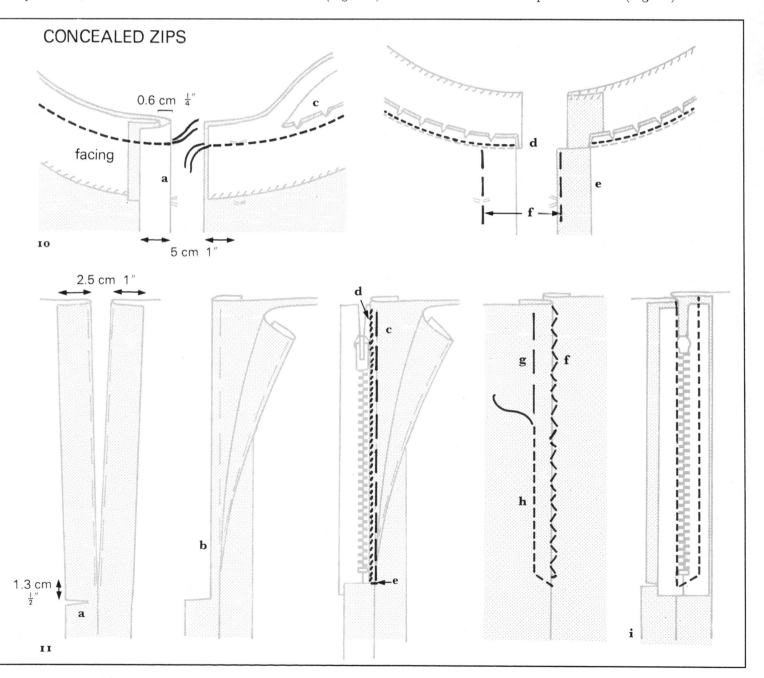

CONCEALED ZIPS

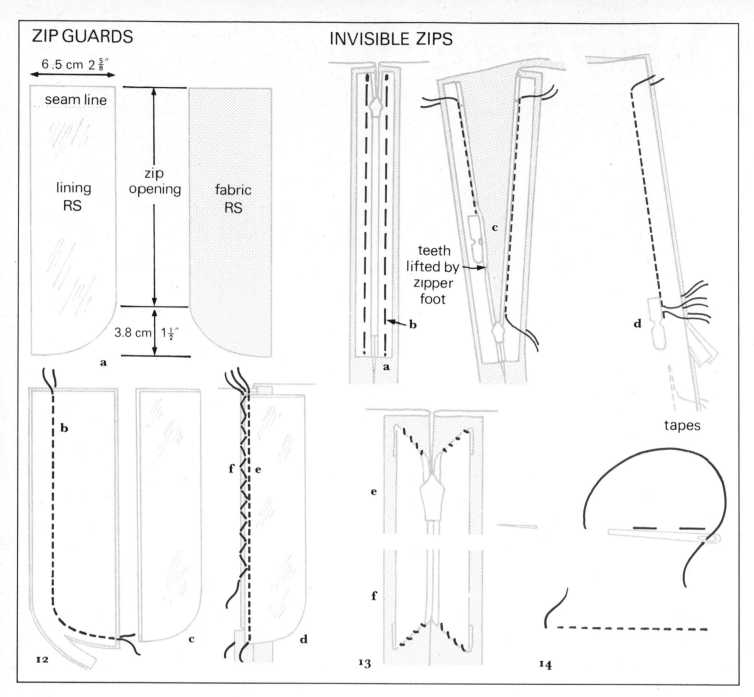

ZIP GUARDS

6.5 cm 2⅝″

seam line

lining RS

zip opening

fabric RS

3.8 cm 1½″

a

b

c

12

f **e**

d

INVISIBLE ZIPS

teeth lifted by zipper foot

b

a

c

d

tapes

e

f

13

14

Place right sides together and stitch the curved side. Turn to the right side and tack around the stitched edge. Press flat. Place the long raw edge to the right hand side zip tape, making sure that the fabric side of the guard is towards the zip. Machine through the guard, zip tape and seam allowance. If the garment is unlined neaten the raw edge.

Invisible zips

These give an opening which looks like a seam, and are ideal except on loose, bulky tweeds where the fibres might be caught by the slide.

After fitting the garment, sew the zip seam, leaving an opening 2.5cm (1in) longer than the zip teeth. Tack and press. The final opening is 2cm (¾in) less than the zip length.

On the wrong side lay the closed zip centrally over the seam with the zip teeth uppermost (Fig. 13a).

Pin and tack through the zip tape and seam allowance only (Fig. 13b).

Remove the seam tacking and open the zip carefully. Keeping the teeth upright, machine through the tape and seam allowance only, stopping when the zipper foot meets the slider. Machine the other side of the zip (Fig. 13c).

Straighten and close zip. Lift zip and seam allowance up and complete the seam still using the zipper foot (Fig. 13d).

Secure the zip tapes to the top by folding the ends outwards and sew to the seam turnings (Fig. 13c).

The tapes at the bottom edge are also sewn to the seam turnings (Fig. 13f).

Half back stitch

Bring the thread up after fastening firmly on the wrong side. Take a tiny stitch back and bring needle up through fabric about 0.3cm (⅛in) forward (Fig. 14).

Other fastenings and belts

Although a well-worked buttonhole is an elegant fastening in its own right, there are times when an even more attractive fastening is required, to be ornamental as well as functional. Fabric button loops, rouleau buttons and frogs come into this category. Belts come into this chapter, too, as they can be considered as more than additional fastenings; sometimes, as in the case of a wrapover coat, they are the only one. Hooks and eyes and press fasteners are neat, additional fastenings, not meant to be seen but to be adding to the trimness of the garment by their invisible closure. Although strong enough to be used alone on very light fabrics, they are usually used in conjunction with stronger fastenings.

Fabric button loops

The basis of loops and frogs is a rouleau, which can be filled with piping cord or left with just the seam allowance of the loop filling the rouleau. To make a rouleau, cut a bias strip about 2.5cm (1in) wide, and the required length of the finished loop (for a row of loops, cut the bias strip about twice the total length) (Fig. 1a).

With right sides together, fold the bias strip in half lengthways. Machine stitch the long edges together the desired distance from the fold: lightweight fabrics need a large seam allowance to fill out the rouleau; heavyweight fabrics need a narrower seam allowance. Trim the strip diagonally at one end to make turning easier and attach a strong thread to this end of the rouleau at the seam (Fig. 1b). Push a blunt needle or bodkin threaded with the strong thread, eye first, through the rouleau. Then pull the thread through to turn the rouleau to the right side (Fig. 1c and d).

There are two ways of making a cord-filled rouleau. One is by cutting a bias strip the required length and width depending on the diameter of the cord. The strip should enclose the cord and have a 1.3cm ($\frac{1}{2}$in) seam allowance. With right sides together fold one narrow end of the bias strip over for about 0.6cm ($\frac{1}{4}$in) and attach the centre of the cord to the flap. Fold the bias strip, wrong side out, over the cord. Stitch close to the cord, using a piping,

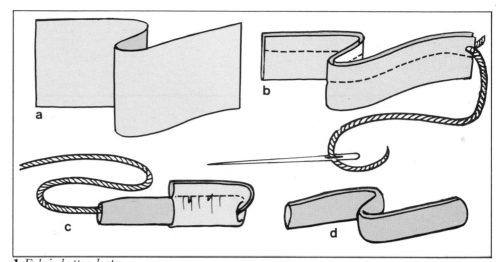

1 *Fabric button loops*

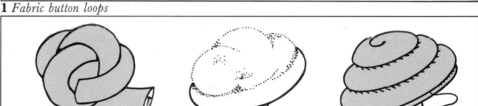

2 *Rouleau buttons*

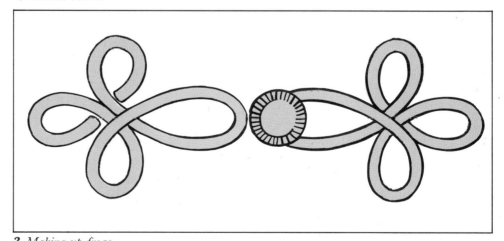

3 *Making up frogs*

4 *Soft tie belts*

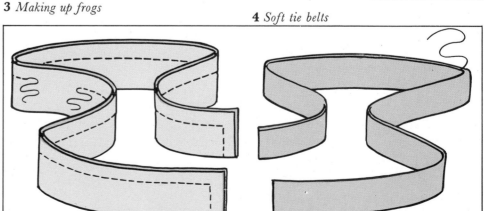

cording or zipper foot on the machine. Trim off excess seam allowance and pull the enclosed cord gently through the strip, working the fabric carefully over the free cord. Cut off excess cord. The other way of making a cord-filled rouleau is to make a plain rouleau tube, trim the seam allowance and turn it to the right side, as described above; then sew the cord to a blunt needle or bodkin and pull the cord through the rouleau. Less cord is used with this method but, unless it is done carefully, the result is not so neat.

If sewing a row of button loops, it is essential that they should be all the same size and evenly spaced. Measure round the button and allow a little extra on each rouleau for sewing it in place. Mark along the length of the edge of the garment where the loops are to be and either cut the number of loops required or leave the strip (if it is long enough) and sew it all in one. If sewing the loops singly, stitch them to the right side of the garment. Stitch the facing over the ends of the loops. When the facing is turned to the inside of the garment, the loops are brought to the edge. With the second method, sew the strip into loops then sew them to the garment as for the first method.

Rouleau buttons

Make a rouleau as described above, about 20cm (8in) long, and twist it into a button shape. Ease the loops into a tight ball and firmly oversew the ends at the back. Cut off excess ends. Or build up an ordinary covered button with a scrap of cotton wool under the fabric, then twist and stitch the rouleau invisibly round the button (Fig. 2).

Frogs

Self-filled or cord-filled rouleaux can be used to make frog fastenings, that are usually coupled with either rouleau buttons or toggles. To make them, twist the rouleau making the fourth loop large enough to go around the button. Make the rouleau for the other side in the same way but in the other direction. Sew one part of the frog to one side of the garment and sew the other part, together with the button or toggle, to correspond on the other side of the garment (Fig. 3).

Hooks and eyes

Hooks should be sewn so that their ends are invisible from the right side and the loops or eyes should be made on the stitching line with a little fabric beyond them as a wrap. Sew hooks and eyes on with loop stitch and work loops for either hooks or buttons by taking three strands of buttonhole twist the length

required (very small for a hook) and
work loop stitch over the strands.

Press fasteners

The socket of a press fastener should be
sewn to the left side of the opening and
the stud part on the right side or over-
laps. Position and sew the stud first
and mark the knob with chalk. Place
both sides of the opening together,
pressing the chalked stud on to the
garment. This will show the position for
the socket. Oversew or buttonhole stitch
three or four stitches in each hole of both
the socket and stud.

Belts

Belts that actually keep garments closed
are soft tie belts and buckled belts.
Other types are just meant as trimmings,
for example a half belt or a quarter belt
set across the back, tabs set into each
side seam. For each of these types,
except the soft tie belt, use two pieces of
fabric the required size, with one piece
of belt stiffening the required length and
width or one piece of fabric three times
the width of the stiffening.

Soft tie belts are made by cutting a
strip of fabric to the required width and
length plus seam allowances, either on
the straight of the grain or on the bias
of the fabric. With right sides together
fold the strip in half and tack along the
raw edge and across both ends. Stitch
from as near the centre along to one end,
turn the corner and stitch across the
end. Repeat from the near centre, going
along in the other direction, leaving an
8cm (3in) gap in the centre of the long
edge. Make sure that the shaping at
each end is identical then turn the belt
to the right side and slipstitch the gap
in the centre to close. Tack around the
stitched edge to hold the belt in shape
and press flat. A very narrow belt is
sometimes difficult to turn through so
sew it with a piece of cord in the same
way as the rouleau strip described
earlier (Fig. 4).

Stiffened belts. For stiffened belts
in one piece use petersham ribbon, iron-
on interfacing, buckram or belt backing
and cut it exactly to the length and
width required for the belt. Cut a piece
of fabric on the straight of the grain a
little longer than the stiffenings and
three times the width. Place and tack
the stiffening into position and catch
stitch it all round the edge. (Or iron it
if it is an iron-on interfacing). On the
shaped end of the belt fold one end of
the fabric narrowly up to the stiffening
and tack, mitring the corners. Do not
turn in the ends at the straight end.

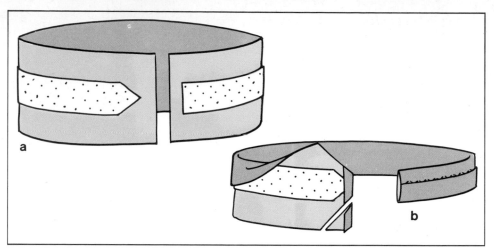

5 *Stiffened belt*

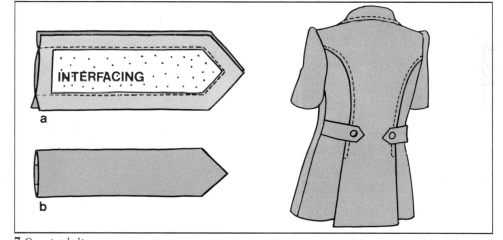

6 *Half belt*

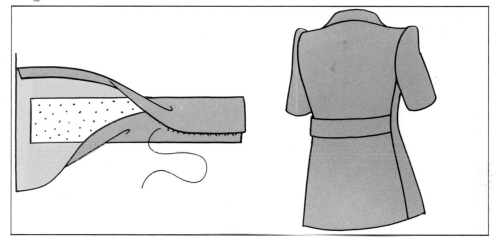

7 *Quarter belt*

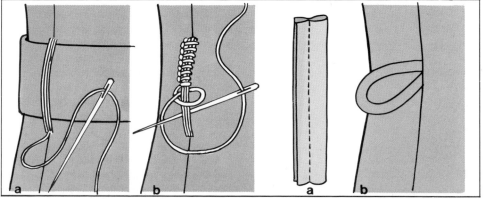

8 *Belt loop*   **9** *Fabric carrier*

47

Take one side of the fabric over the stiffening and tack. Turn in the raw edge of the other side of the fabric and fold it over the stiffening to cover the raw edge of the first side of the fabric. Hem all along the ends and centre of the belt (Fig. 5).

Belts in two pieces. Tack the interfacing to the wrong side of one section of the belt. With right sides together tack the belt facing to the belt and interfacing. Stitch the long edges, and stitch one end into a point. Leave the other free. Turn the belt to the right side through this end tack around the stitched edge and press flat. If attaching a buckle, do not finish off the straight end of the belt. Thread this through the buckle, turn it to the wrong side and herringbone stitch it to the back of the belt. If not attaching a buckle, turn in each raw edge of the end of the belt and slipstitch the edges together. Sew hooks and eyes or press fasteners to close.

Half belts. For a half belt across the back, which is usually set over a plain back of a coat or dress, make up the stiffened belt to the size required but leave both ends unstitched. Sew the belt into the side seams of the garment, with raw edges level.

Quarter belts For a quarter belt set into the side seams, usually set where there are two seams or pleats down the back, make up a stiffened belt with one pointed end (perhaps with a buttonhole at this end). Leave the other end unstitched. Repeat with the point end (and the buttonhole) at the other end. Set each tab into a side seam so that the buttonhole comes over the seam or pleat down the back. Sew a button on to the seam or pleat at each side to correspond with the buttonholes. A strap cuff is made and sewn in the same way, into the sleeve seam, pointing towards the back. For a quarter belt at the back, usually set across the back of a coat with shaped seams, make up a stiffened belt with straight ends, sewing from near the centre of one long edge, across one end, along the other long side, across the other end and back down the first long side, leaving a gap in the centre of the seam through which to turn the belt. Layer seam allowances, turn the belt to the right side and slipstitch the opening to close. Press. Make buttonholes and topstitch all round if required.
Place the belt centrally across the back and sew on buttons to correspond with buttonholes at the shaped seams (Fig. 6).

Belt loops and carriers
A loop should be made no wider than the belt it is to carry. Pin the belt in position (on a tall figure, the belt will fall better just below the waist, on a short figure, it will look better above the waist). Using double buttonhole twist, make several strands across the belt at the side seams. Remove the belt and work loop stitch over strands (Fig. 7).
A fabric carrier is made by cutting a piece of material 1.3 to 2cm ($\frac{1}{2}$ to $\frac{3}{4}$in) wide on the straight of the grain. With right sides together, fold it in half lengthways and machine stitch 0.6cm ($\frac{1}{4}$in) from the raw edges. Turn it to the

Above. *Frogging can be used to great effect especially as a front fastening on heavier fabrics, such as this thick winter coat.*

right side and press it. Place the loop in position on the right side of the fabric so that the ends of the loop overlap the stitching line by 0.6cm ($\frac{1}{4}$in). Place the other side of the garment, right sides together, enclosing the loop, and sew the seam in the usual way, making two rows of stitching across the loop. Obviously, the seam will have to be a plain one and not a French or a flat-fell seam (Fig. 8).

Trimmings

Braiding can be worked either in rows or following a traced-off pattern (soutache). It should first be tacked then slipstitched in place, along both long edges. For a traced pattern, pierce a hole in the fabric with a stiletto at the beginning of the design, and push the end of the braid through to the wrong side and sew the end securely in place. On the right side, using fine silk and stab stitch through the centre of the braid sew it to the garment following the design. Finish the end of the braid off as started.

Lace to be used as insertion should be tacked in place with the wrong side placed to the right side of the fabric, then the edges sewn finely, but strongly, to the background fabric. The fabric behind the lace should then be cut away, leaving a very narrow seam allowance. This seam allowance should then be loop stitched to prevent it from fraying. If a lace edging is to be sewn on as a frill, mark the lace into an even number of sections and divide the edge of the garment that is to be trimmed into an equal number. Draw up the edge of the lace and pin and tack it to the fabric, regulating the fullness according to the division. Oversew the two edges together on the wrong side.

Scallops are an attractive finish to the hem of a dress and can be made simply with a template cut from card, shaped from the edge of saucer or with a compass. Make the template the shape of two scallops. Lay the template on the right side of the fabric and mark round it with chalk, moving the template all along to be scalloped. Do not cut round the scallops yet. They have to be neatened first with either bias binding or with a facing. To face, cut a bias strip of the fabric a little deeper than the scallops. Mark the scallop on the wrong side of this fabric using the template. Tack the bias strip to the fabric, right sides together, and stitch all round the scalloped line. Cut round the scallops, leaving 0.6cm ($\frac{1}{4}$in) seam allowance. Notch the curves and clip into the corners. Turn the facing to the wrong side and tack round the stitched edge easing the scallops into shape. Press flat. Turn under the edge of the facing and slipstitch it to the garment. If using bias binding, stitch the bias binding all round the edge of the scalloped line, allowing it to fall easily round the scallops themselves, stretching it at the

inner curves. Turn the binding over and hem it to the first line of stitching, making a neat little pleat at each point.

Piping is sewn round the edges of sleeves, collars, yokes and other highlights of a garment. Piped seams can be stunning if they are in a strong contrasting colour.

Make a piped rouleau by folding a strip of fabric around a length of piping cord and sewing as close to the cord as

Above. *Decorative braiding was used to provide a contrast colour to this design.*

possible. Place the rouleau between the two parts of the garment to be piped, with right sides of fabric together and the raw edges of the piped rouleau level with the raw edges of the garment. Tack and machine stitch as close as possible to the cord. Ease the piping on an outside corner or curve and stretch it on an inner curve.

Pleats

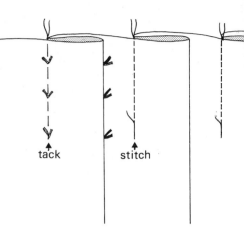

1 *Stitch knife pleats on wrong side*

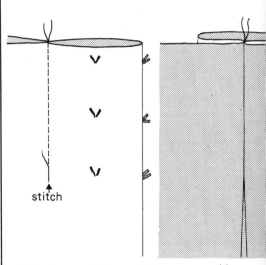

2 *For inverted pleats, stitch on wrong side*

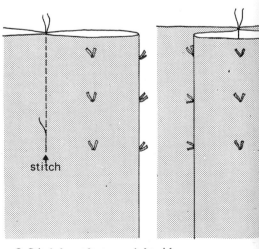

3 *Stitch box pleats on right side.*

Pleats

Pleats are set into a garment as part of a design and to allow more room within the garment for ease of movement. Wide knife pleats arranged in groups, inverted pleats and box pleats are often set in skirts to give extra width at the hemline, making it easier to walk. Pleats must always be evenly formed and hang straight. To do this they must be held firmly and flat and enough fabric must have been allowed for them. The amount of fabric used for each pleat is three times its finished width so a 2.5cm (1in) pleat requires an 8cm (3in) width of material. Check the width before tacking. The sharp edges depend on accurate placing and careful tacking. Always work on a flat surface such as a table, never on the knee. Pin each pleat carefully, following the balance lines. Where pleats are left to hang loosely from the top of a skirt, they are finally secured in place by being held in a waistband. It is only necessary in this case to tack the pleats and leave them to be held later.

Knife pleats can be arranged in groups or spaced evenly all round a skirt so that they meet, edge to edge. Where there are several tight pleats, as in a kilt or across the back of a skirt, tack across the pleats evenly every 10 to 15cm (4 to 5in). If stitching from the right side of the fabric, machine close to each pleat and make sure that this stitching is kept evenly spaced from the pleat edge on all pleats. If stitching from the wrong side, machine on the stitching line of the pleat for the length required, then fold back the upper layer of fabric to cover the stitches (Fig. 1).

Inverted pleats are formed by two knife pleats, one folded one way and one folded the other way to meet the first. Machine on the wrong side 0.3cm ($\frac{1}{8}$in) away from the edge of each side of the pleat in each case, working around the end of the pleat, either in a curved, pointed or squared-off line. If the fabric is very thick, the seam allowance at the top of the pleat may be cut away to reduce bulk (Fig. 2).

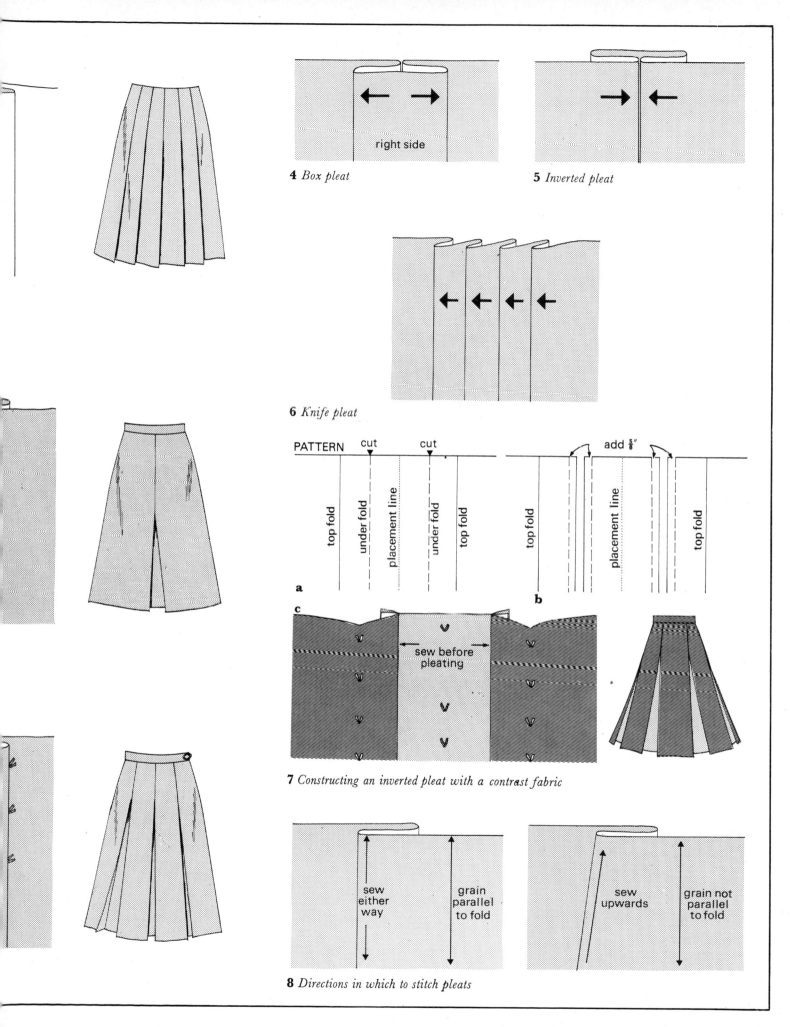

4 *Box pleat*

5 *Inverted pleat*

6 *Knife pleat*

PATTERN

cut   cut   add ⅝″

top fold / under fold / placement line / under fold / top fold

top fold / placement line / top fold

a   **b**

c   sew before pleating

7 *Constructing an inverted pleat with a contrast fabric*

sew either way / grain parallel to fold

sew upwards / grain not parallel to fold

8 *Directions in which to stitch pleats*

Box pleats look like inverted pleats viewed from the back. Folding two knife pleats towards the back of the fabric instead of the front forms a box pleat. Working from the right side of the fabric, stitch 0.3cm ($\frac{1}{8}$in) from the outside edge of the box pleat on thin fabrics or 0.6cm ($\frac{1}{4}$in) from the edge on heavier materials. This will require making a point at the end of the pleat towards the edge of the fabric. If working from the wrong side of the fabric, machine on the stitching line of the pleat, for the length required. Open out the fabric and arrange the fold line to flatten out underneath the machining (Fig. 3).

Pleats hidden in seams

Sometimes it is more economical in cutting out the fabric, to allow for a seam to come within a pleat, so that it is hidden from view when the garment is being worn.

Strengthening the ends of pleats

The end of the pleat is always a point of a strain and some strengthening is therefore necessary. This can be in the form of a bar tack (or a "stay" of buckram or spare fabric). The bar tack is worked after the pleats are sewn, the stay is sewn before. Cut a 4cm ($1\frac{1}{2}$in) square of fabric and overcast the edges all round. Tack it to the wrong side of the garment where the stitching of the pleat will end or turn so that, when the pleat is sewn, the stay will be caught in place. On thick fabrics arrowheads are often used at the bottom of the stitching on inverted pleats. These are a decorative, as well as a strengthening finish to a pleat so they must be neatly worked. Use silk buttonhole twist in a colour to match the fabric and work the arrowhead this way. Take the needle from the right side of the fabric to the wrong side at the right-hand side, make the sides about 1.3cm ($\frac{1}{2}$in) long and bring the needle through from the wrong side of the fabric to the right side at the left-hand side.

With knife-pleated kilts, a length of straight seam binding must be stitched across the top of the pleats to hold them firm, and is caught to each pleat with two or three cross stitches.

Tucks

Tucks are narrow folds of fabric stitched, always on the straight of grain, parallel to the fold all the way along their length. In dressmaking, tucks are usually made on the straight of the grain, 1.3cm ($\frac{1}{2}$in) wide although, in lingerie making, they are usually 0.6cm ($\frac{1}{4}$in). Tucks are pressed flat and usually

away from the centre of the garment. Each tuck, in the same way as a pleat, needs three times its width of fabric to be allowed for it. They are rarely worked singly, usually in groups of two or more. They are a decorative way of controlling fullness, for example, at the shoulder line of a blouse or dress. When sewing by hand, work on the underside of the tuck; when working by machine, sew on the upper side. This brings the better side of the stitching to the top in each case. Again, as in pleating, tucks must be worked carefully and attractively and the whole idea is decorative as well as functional.

Types of tuck
Pin tucks
These are very narrow tucks which can be arranged in groups or evenly spaced. They can be made automatically on many of the modern twin-needle sewing machines, which can also raise and cord the tucks, or they can be made on most other sewing machines by accurately top stitching 0.3cm ($\frac{1}{8}$in) away from the fold edge of the fabric (Fig. 1). Suitable fabrics are: Nun's veiling, voile, cotton lawn, Terylene lawn, silk, chiffon, cotton and lightweight wool.

Wide tucks
These are made in a similar way to pin tucks but instead of stitching 0.3cm ($\frac{1}{8}$in) away from the fold edge, the stitching is usually 0.6cm-1.3cm ($\frac{1}{4}$in-$\frac{1}{2}$in) away from the fold edge.
The depth and spacing of these tucks will depend on the design of the garment, the type of fabric being tucked and the finished effect required. So experiment with some of the fabric being used before deciding on the depth of the tuck and the spacing required. Then make a double notched tuck guide to the required measurements. Suitable fabrics are the same as for pin tucks plus lightweight jersey fabrics.

Corded tucks
Enclose the cord in the tuck and stitch using a cording or zipper foot on the sewing machine.
If a slippery fabric is being used, it is advisable to tack the cord in place before stitching (Fig. 2).
Suitable fabrics: corded tucks are best made on fabrics which are dry cleanable rather than washable because when the cord is inserted into the tuck it tends to be a little bulky, and if worked on a washable fabric, drying might be a problem.

Cross tucks
These are a variation of normal pin

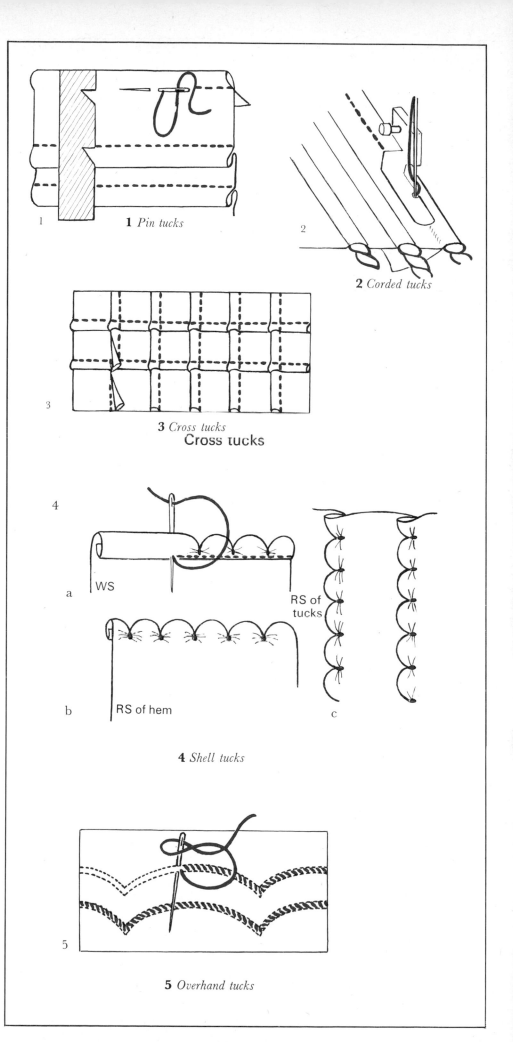

1 *Pin tucks*

2 *Corded tucks*

3 *Cross tucks*
Cross tucks

a   WS

b   RS of hem

RS of tucks

c

4 *Shell tucks*

5 *Overhand tucks*

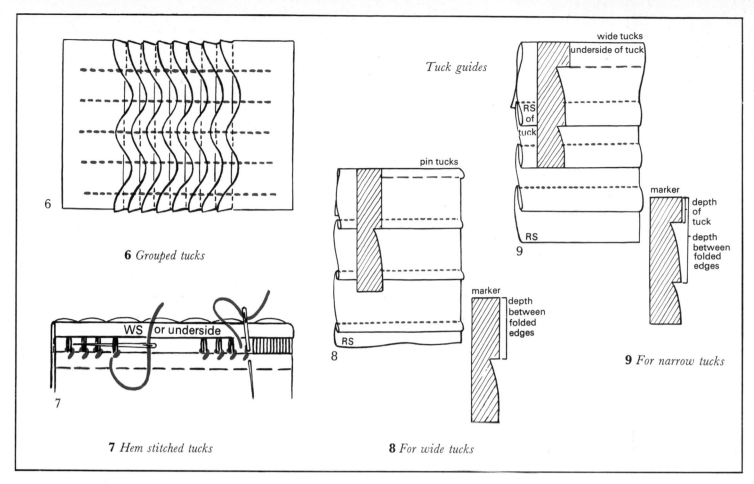

6 *Grouped tucks*

Tuck guides

7 *Hem stitched tucks*

8 *For wide tucks*

9 *For narrow tucks*

tucks and when arranged in groups they can be most a attractive form of decoration on a garment.

Cross tucks consist of a second row of tucks made across a normal group of pin tucks. First work all the tucks across in one direction, then work the crossing tucks. Extra care must be taken with the second group of tucks to avoid the fabric slipping and to ensure that each crossing is true (Fig. 3).

Suitable fabrics: cross tucks are most effective when worked on fine fabrics such as lawn, lurex, voile and chiffon.

Shell tucks

Crease the tuck and tack along the folded edge. Mark the length of each shell with a small dot at intervals. The length of the shell should be about twice the depth of the tuck. Work running stitches along the tuck, and on reaching each dot, take two stitches over the tuck, drawing the thread up tight to form the shell pattern (Fig. 4).

Shell tucks can be used in groups, singly, running vertically or horizontally. Suitable fabrics: these tucks are most successful when worked on very fine fabric such as lawn, cheesecloth, chiffon

Left. *Pleats can be both decorative and functional, giving a smart finish to a skirt as well as more room for movement.*

or any fine fabric which is normally difficult to work on and produce a neat finish.

Overhand tucks

Mark lines for the tiny ticks and work neat overhead stitches along the lines using either a self of contrast colour sewing thread (Fig. 5).

These tucks can be worked in straight lines or in scollops. Fabrics suitable for these designs are the same as for pin tucks.

Grouped tucks

Make several lines of tucks close together and press them all in one direction at the top. Stitch across the tucks in the direction they have been pressed. Then turn the tucks in the opposite direction and at the desired interval, stitch across them in the new direction. The tucks are turned alternately in this way until the required area has been completed (Fig. 6).

Suitable fabrics: this is a simple method of producing a decorative raised pattern on a plain fabric and because they are stitched alternatively from one direction to another, a striking effect can be obtained by using a fabric with a rich pile to produce a shaded texture.

Hem stitched tucks

Mark the fold edge of the tuck along

the grain of the fabric with tacking stitches. Draw out one or two threads for the finished width of the tuck at an even distance from either side of the fold line. Tack the tuck along the fold line and work the hem stitching from the underside of the tuck. Press the tuck flat in position and measure the distance to the fold line of the next tuck as shown for wide tucks. Mark the fold line with tacking stitches and repeat as for the first tuck (Fig. 7).

Suitable fabrics: lightweight fabrics of a loose even weave where the threads can be withdrawn easily.

Tuck guide
For wide tucks

Cut a 10cm x 2.3cm (4in x 1in) strip of stiff cardboard, squaring the corners accurately. Measure the width of the tuck required down from the top and make a 0.6cm ($\frac{1}{4}$in) cut, parallel to the top. Make a second cut diagonally from below the first to make a triangular notch. Make another straight cut away from the first (the distance required between the tuck and the stitching), again notching out a diagonal (Fig. 8).

For pin tucks

Cut a rectangle of cardboard as for wide tucks. Mark the distance required between the fold edges and cut out a notch as described above (Fig. 9).

Pockets

1 *Positioning of pockets*

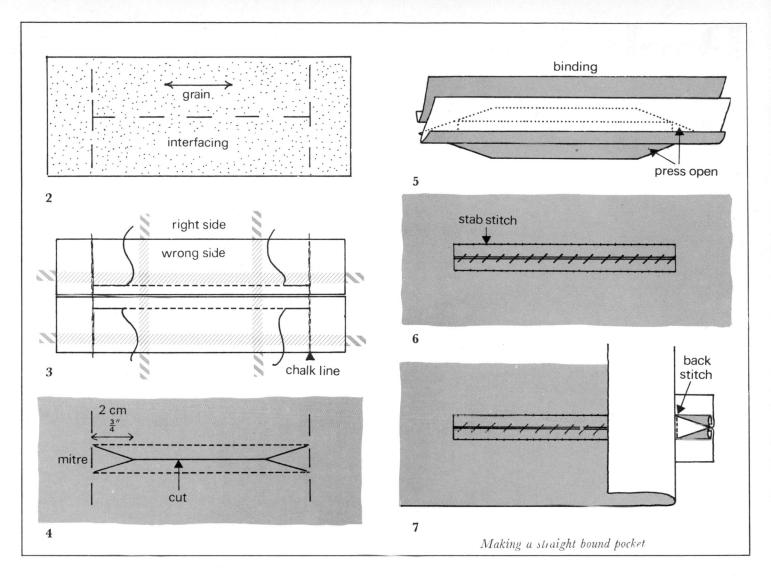

Making a straight bound pocket

Give your sewing a professional finish with perfect pockets. First choose an unusual fabric, an attractive trim, or exciting buttons, to bring a new dimension to functional pockets and turn them into the highlight of your garment.

Pocket position

To decide where to place the pocket, pin the pattern pieces together and either try it on yourself or on a dressmaker's shape. Cut paper shapes the size of the proposed flap or patch, and try various positions on the pattern until a pleasing result is obtained. Pin in place and mark a position on the pattern (Fig. 1a to f).

The average pocket length for a dress is 11.5cm (4½in) to 12.5cm (5½in) and a patch can be any size or shape, to suit the dress design.

All pockets are backed by interfacing, tacked on to the wrong side of the garment.

Cut this with the grain falling along the line of the pocket and where possible take it into a seam for added strength.

Bound pockets

Bound pockets are made initially in the same way as bound buttonholes and can look most effective if a contrasting fabric is used. They can also be shaped, as opposed to straight, if it is felt that this enhances the design.

Method of working straight bound pocket

Tack the pocket line through the fabric and interfacing (Fig. 2).

Cut two bindings 5cm (2in) wide by pocket length plus 3.8cm (1½in) and position right side down on the right side of the garment with the edges meeting the tacked line, matching patterns if appropriate.

Tack to the garment and chalk mark the ends of the pocket opening.

Working from the right side, stitch along the pocket length on each binding, overstitching for 1.3cm (½in) at each end. The lines should extend 0.6cm (¼in) each side of the pocket line (Fig. 3).

Working on the wrong side, cut along the pocket line making 2cm (¾in) mitres at the corners. Do not cut the pipes (Fig. 4).

Pull the bindings through the opening to the wrong side. Press the seams open and the mitres away from the opening (Fig. 5).

Working on the right side, adjust the bindings into even folds and oversew to close (Fig. 6). Stab stitch as shown.

Fold the garment back and back stitch through the binding and mitre as close to the fold as possible (Fig. 7).

Shaped bound pockets

Mark the pocket position carefully and make sure that the interfacing is large enough to be under the pocket stitching. Cut one patch of fabric suitable for the pocket shape, using self or contrast fabric. Place right side down on right side of garment, watching the grain carefully. Tack along the pocket line (Fig. 8).

Stitch carefully at equal distances from the tacking; the width depends on how you would like the pocket to look, but should not be less than 1.3cm (½in) (Fig. 9).

Cut through the patch to make the binding (Fig. 10).

On the wrong side, cut through the garment along the pocket line, mitring the corners (Fig. 11).
Finish as for a straight bound pocket, snipping any curved seams.

Flap pockets

Having decided the shape of your flap, cut out a paper pattern without turnings (Fig. 12a and b).
From the same or contrasting fabric, cut one flap to this pattern plus turnings as shown (Fig. 13a). Cut one flap of lining to match (Fig. 13b).
Cut one piece of interfacing to the exact shape of the finished flap (Fig. 13c).
Cut one binding piece as for bound straight pockets.

Making the flap

Place the interfacing to the wrong side of the flap and catch stitch all round (Fig. 14a). Fold the turnings on to the interfacing, snipping curves or mitring corners. Herringbone stitch into place (Fig. 14b). Press well.
Place the lining to the wrong side of the flap. Fold the turnings slightly inside the edge of the flap and hem (Fig. 15).
Press well and draw a chalk line on the right side at the sewing line (Fig. 16).

Method of working flap pocket

Tack the pocket line through the fabric and interfacing. Place the chalk line on the flap to the pocket line and machine. Overstitch the ends for 1.3cm (½in) (Fig. 17).
Fold the flap seam up and stitch the bottom binding in place, overstitching the ends (Fig. 18).
From the wrong side, cut as for the bound pocket (Fig. 4).
Turn the flap seam allowance through the opening to the wrong side, leaving the flap on the right side. Press this up and the mitres away from the opening (Fig. 19). Treat the binding as for the bound pocket (Fig. 20).

Lining for bound and flap pockets

Cut a backing for the pocket in self fabric, 7.5cm (3in) deep and the length of the binding. Stitch to the top binding or flap seam allowance as near as possible to the original stitching line. For added strength, stitch again 1.3cm (½in) above the first row (Fig. 21).
For each pocket cut two pieces of lining 10cm (4in) deep and the length of the binding. Stitch one piece of lining to the lower edge of the backing and the other to the bottom binding.
Round off the lower corners and stitch all round, catching in the mitres.

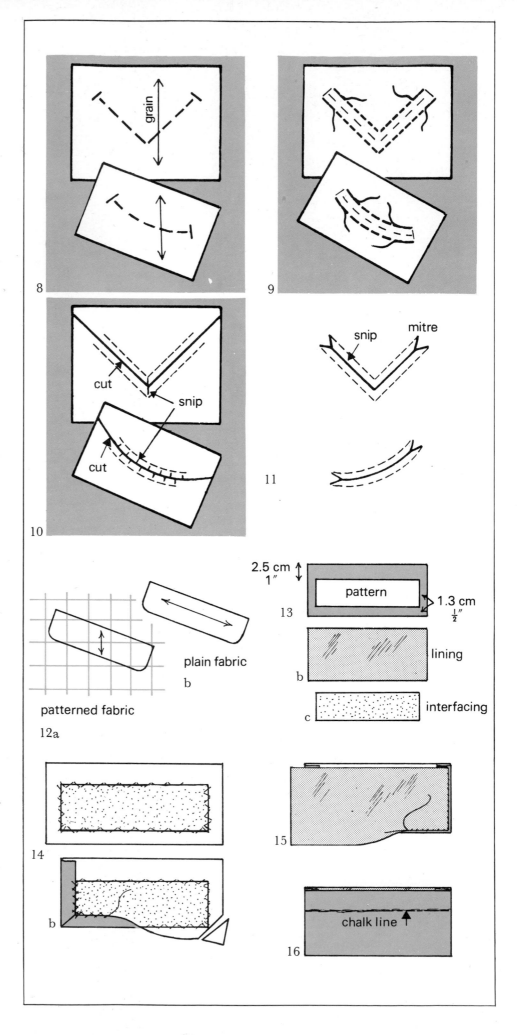

If this is difficult, use a machine with a zipper foot (Fig. 22).

Patch pockets

Cut out a pocket shape in fabric with 1.5cm ($\frac{5}{8}$in) seam allowance plus an extra 2.5cm (1in) at the top edge. Cut the exact pocket shape in interfacing.

Cut the lining 5cm (2in) shorter than the pocket (Fig. 23).

Method of working patch pocket

Make the pocket as for the flap (Figs. 14 and 15), making a 2.5cm (1in) hem at the top. Press well.

Apply the pocket to the garment by top stitching or ladder stitch (Fig. 24a and b).

Pocket in a seam

Mark the pocket position on the pattern pieces. When laying out, allow room for extra seam allowance to be cut 5cm (2in) longer than the pocket length (Fig. 25).

The lining shape is obtained by drawing in one curve around your hand, allowing reasonable room. Cut the shape in lining material plus 1.5cm ($\frac{5}{8}$in) turnings (Fig. 25).

Method of working pocket in seam

Place the right side of the lining to the right side of the garment and machine 1.5cm ($\frac{5}{8}$in) from the straight edge as shown. Machine again 1.3cm ($\frac{1}{2}$in) from the edge to give extra strength (Fig. 26).

Press the lining and the seam away from the garment.

Place the garment pieces right sides together, matching the pocket markings. Tack and machine down the seam, round the pocket and continue to hem (Fig. 27).

Neaten the lining.

Snip the garment as shown (Fig. 28). Press the seams open and the pocket towards the front of the garment.

Decorative ideas

Pockets need not be purely functional—they can also be used to add some colour or to give an individual touch to an otherwise plain or simple garment.

With patch pockets, for instance, this is fairly easy to do. Differing colours, fabrics or shapes can be used and applied in the usual way.

With other types of pockets it is more difficult. Topstitching in a contrasting colour around the edges of the pocket can often produce an unusual effect. An applique patch or a button trim can also be used to highlight or add some colour to a flap or seam pocket.

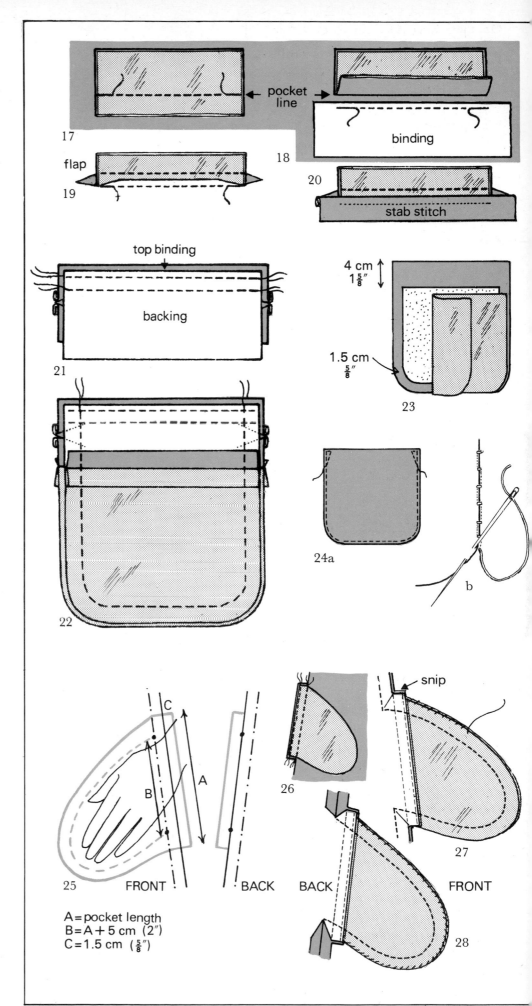

17
flap
19
18
pocket line
binding
20
stab stitch
top binding
backing
21
22
4 cm
1 $\frac{5}{8}$"
1.5 cm
$\frac{5}{8}$"
23
24a
b
25 FRONT
A = pocket length
B = A + 5 cm (2")
C = 1.5 cm ($\frac{5}{8}$")
C
B
A
BACK
26
snip
27
BACK
FRONT
28

Hems

Beautifully finished hems are most important as they provide a professional finish to all the care given in the making of a garment. The length is dictated by fashion to a certain extent, but it must be right both for the garment and for the particular figure.

Wearing appropriate shoes, check the length of a garment before a mirror and always wear the jacket when looking at a suit skirt to see that the proportion of jacket to skirt is correct.

General points
Hem length

There are various ways to get the right hem length:

From the back neck, measure the length of the pattern and adjust if necessary. After cutting out, tailor tack along the hem line and pin the hem up to the line when fitting (Fig. 1a and b).

Place a dress of the right length on a hanger with the new dress over it. Pin up the new hem to match (Fig. 2).

Ask a friend to measure up from the ground and mark the line with pins (Fig. 3).

Use a skirt marker. Be careful here measure 1.3cm (½in) longer than needed to avoid the possibility of the chalk marking the fabric permanently. Turn up 1.3cm (½in) above the chalk line. (Fig. 4).

Preparation before neatening

Trace tack along the hem fold and un-pin (Fig. 5). Most hems are 5 to 6.5cm (2 to 2½in) deep, so trim evenly to the required depth (Fig. 6). Exceptions are for blouses, 2.5cm (1in); faced hems 1.3cm (½in); long skirts of fine fabric 1.3cm (½in).

Trim all seams to 0.6cm (¼in) between the hem line and the hem edge (Fig. 7).

Hem neatening

For non-fray fabrics oversew or zigzag along the cut edge. For fraying fabrics use one of the following methods:

Zigzag 0.6cm (¼in) away from the cut edge and trim to the machining. For straight hem lines, edge with straight binding. For curved or bias edges, ease the hem and edge with bias binding. For fine cottons (mainly children's clothes and summer dresses), fold under the raw edge for 1.3cm (½in) (Fig. 8). For pleats which are seamed, the seam turnings are snipped the hem depth above the hem line and pressed open below the snip. Above the snip, the

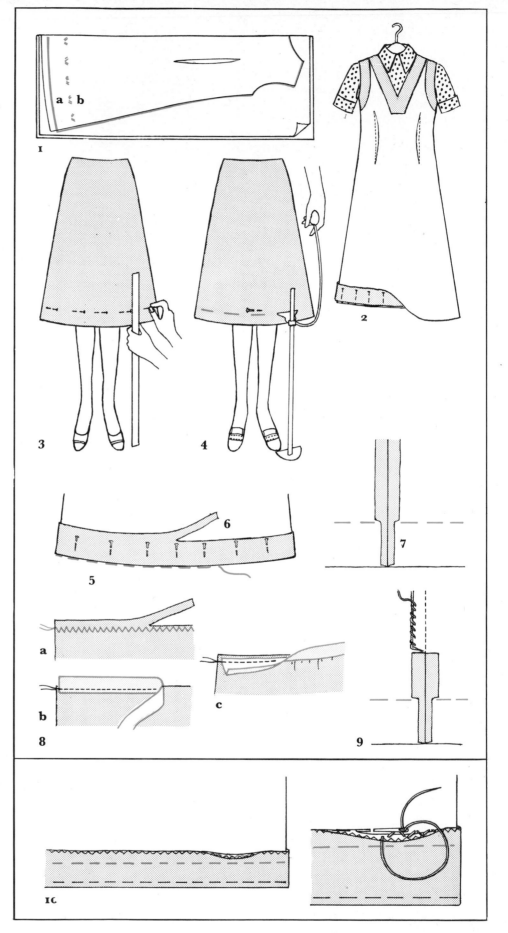

turnings are neatened and pressed together (Fig. 9).

After neatening the raw edge, press it, making sure it is away from the body of

Right. *Turning up a hem on a very flared skirt can cause great problems. It is often simpler if finished with a very narrow faced hem.*

the garment.

Fold the hem up on the tacked line, slip a piece of card or brown paper inside the fold and press well. Use a damp cloth rather than a steam iron as it is easier to control the amount of steam this way. Tack through the folded edge to keep it firmly in place.

Types of hem
Plain: this is used for absolutely straight hems such as those on skirts and trousers. Tack the hem 1.3cm (½in) below the neatened edge. Stitch into place using invisible hemming stitch (Fig. 10).

Slightly flared—A-line skirts and flared trousers: after tacking the fold, run a gathering thread 0.6cm (¼in) below the neatened edge. Pull up the gathering thread until the seams match and the hem lies in place. Ease out the fullness evenly (Fig. 11a).
For fabrics which will shrink, press as shown and invisible hem stitch into place (Fig. 11b).
For fabrics which will not shrink, attach bias binding, stretching it slightly. Fold the binding over the raw edge and slip stitch in place (Fig. 11c).

Very flared skirts: it is not easy to make a deep hem for these, so they are usually finished either with a narrow or a faced hem.

Narrow hem for lightweight fabrics: Cut the hem depth to 2cm (¾in). Do not neaten the edge. Run a gathering thread 0.6cm (¼in) from the cut edge. Turn under 0.6cm (¼in) and pull the gathering thread so it lies easily to the skirt. Slip stitch the hem through the fold (Fig. 12a).

Narrow hem for heavier fabrics: Cut the hem depth to 1.3cm (½in) and neaten the edge by oversewing or zig-zag stitch. Press the hem up over paper and stitch with invisible hemming stitch (Fig. 12b).

Faced hem for all fabrics: if extra bulk is not desirable, then lining or net can be used for the facing fabric.
Cut a 5cm (2in) shaped facing from the skirt pattern. Sew the seams together and neaten the shorter edge. Place the facing to the right side of the skirt hem and stitch. Turn up and press. Sew the facing to the skirt with invisible hemming stitch (Fig. 13).

Rolled hem for sheer fabrics: trim the hem to 0.6cm (¼in). Turn under 0.3cm (⅛in) and either slipstitch hem or machine (Fig. 14).

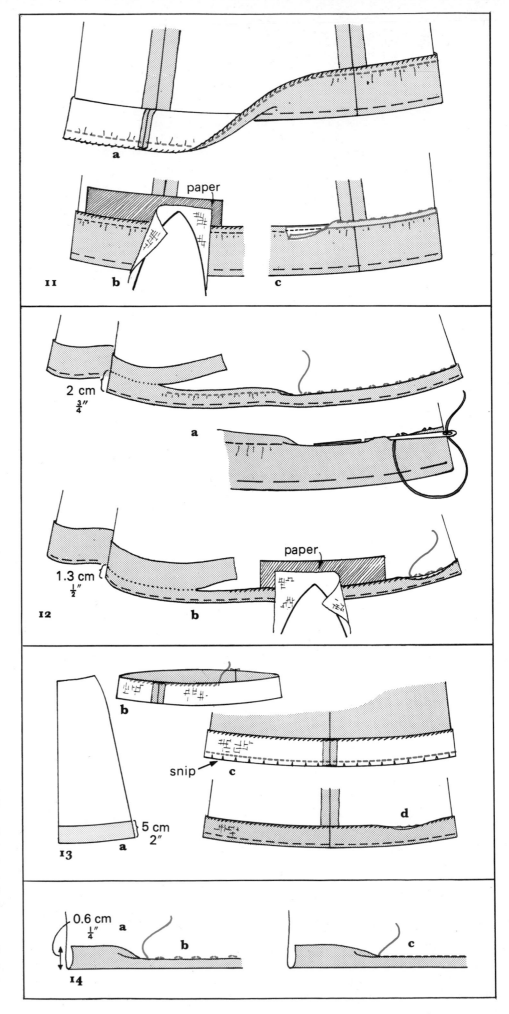

Pressing

For a perfectly finished piece of work, the garment should be pressed at every stage; each seam, each dart and buttonhole should be pressed as it is sewn. Bear in mind that pressing is not ironing. Ironing is a smoothing over; pressing is a lifting up and putting down of the iron at points where the garment needs it. Work in the direction of the grain of the fabric at all times and be sure to test for the correct temperature on a spare piece of fabric before starting. Take time over the job; this is a process that must not be hurried. Have the working surface ready and all the equipment to hand before starting. The ironing board should be well covered with a blanket or several layers of thick fabric.

Pressing cloths must be damp and not wet as the latter will mark the fabric.

As the iron is lifted after each pressing, quickly remove the damp cloth and hold a tailor's clapper or wooden pressing block firmly over the pressed section for some seconds. This helps to set the seam ensuring a nice crisp fold. Press and clap the folds of pleats, hems, darts, pockets and edges. Press seams open over a seam roll. This is improvised very simply by wrapping a tea towel round and round a rolling pin or by rolling up a piece of old blanket very tightly and sewing up the edge with herringbone stitch. Having a number of different sized seam rolls is useful: for example, a long one made from a discarded roller from a roller blind is ideal for long seams on dresses and coats. It is a nuisance and does not give such a good finished result to keep moving along a long seam. A pencil makes a

splendid seam roll for 'fiddly' seams.

To make a tailor's ham for pressing curved seams, cut four egg-shaped pieces of calico or close-weave cotton, 40cm (16in) long, 30cm (13in) wide at the top, graduating to 20cm (8in) wide at the bottom. With right sides together. sew two of the ovals together, leaving a 10cm (4in) wide gap. Turn the ham to the right side and fill very firmly indeed with chopped-up rags. Hem the opening securely to close. Repeat with the other two ovals and cover the ham with it. Slipstitch the opening.

Pressing flat seams

Remove all tacking stitches and lay the garment with the right side of the seam placed down over a pressing roll, making sure that the rest of the garment is well supported (on the back of a chair

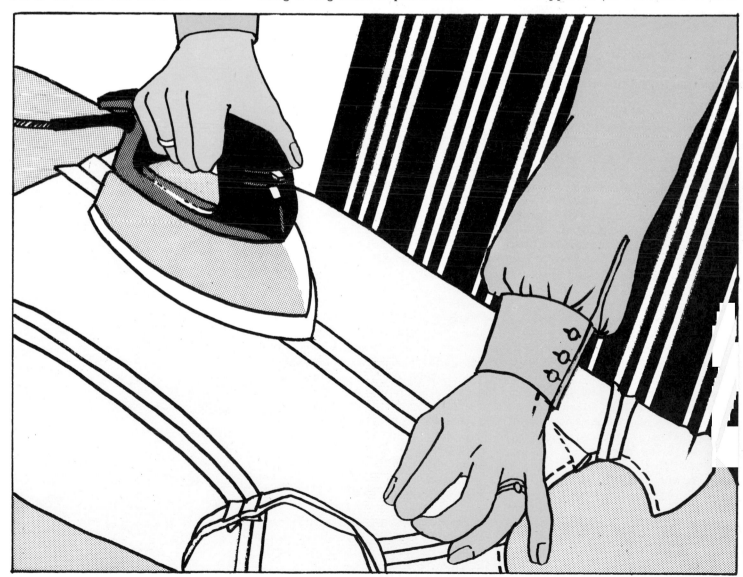

perhaps). Press seams open flat with the point of the iron. Look at the right side of the garment to make sure that the seam line is flat before pressing with a damp cloth and clapping on the wrong side. Pressing over a seam roll avoids the edge of the seam being pressed through to leave imprints on the right side of the fabric but if pressing on an ironing board and imprints do show through, these can usually be removed by running the iron lightly under the seam allowance (not in the case of rayons or silks, however, which should always be pressed over a seam roll) or by placing strips of spare material under the seam allowance.

Eased seams

Where a seam has been eased or fabric is to be moulded, shrink away the fabric as follows. Lay the garment flat on the ironing board, right side down. Shrink away the ease with the point of the iron and a damp pressing cloth. Open the seam, lay it over a pressing roll and shrink the eased seam edge. While the fabric is damp, stretch the uneased edge. Finally press and clap the seam.

Darts

After stitching the dart, cut along the fold on thick fabrics, as near to the point as possible. Lay the dart, right side down over a ham. Press and clap the dart open. On thinner fabric, do not slash the dart but press it down, never pressing beyond the point so that fabric outside the dart will not be creased. Press darts at neck, shoulder and waistline towards the centre front or centre back. This gives a softer appearance to the garment. Press underarm darts towards the waist and elbow darts towards the wrist, so that each dart follows the direction in which the garment will hang while being worn.

Pleats

Press each fold on its underside, withdrawing the tacking stitches as you go, so that the thread makes no impression.

Edges

Press firmly at edges, especially where a separate facing has been attached. Place sections of the edge of the garment on the ironing board and press, taking care not to stretch the edge.

Sleeve heads

Seam allowances of sleeves are not trimmed nor snipped but pressed on the wrong side towards the sleeve. In this way, the sleeve and armhole seam allowances provide support for the head of the sleeve and give it a good shape.

Place a ham or rolled up towel inside the sleeve head, and press the seam bit by bit, pressing with the point of the iron.

Sleeves

Short sleeves can be pressed on a sleeve board but long sleeves should be pressed over a pressing pad, to avoid creases.

Collars

When the collar has been joined to the garment, lift the collar and press the neck join from underneath the collar. Then fold the collar into the rolled position and place it over a sleeve board or ham. Press up to the roll of the collar but not over it.

Hems

Press the edge of the hem but do not press over the stitching line as this will show through to the right side of the garment and leave an ugly line.

Final pressing

Whereas it is essential for all previous processes to have been pressed on the wrong side of the garment, as each stage was completed, the final pressing can sometimes be done on the right side. Never press on the right side without a pressing cloth, however, in case the fabric ends up with a mark or a shine but, for top pressing, the pressing cloth can be a dry, and not a damp, one. Follow this order for the final press: sleeves and cuffs, front edges up to the collar, collar, pockets and tabs, shoulders and sleeve heads, finishing off with the main body of the garment: bodice first and then the skirt. A cool iron may be run over the lining afterwards if necessary.

Some difficult fabrics need special pressing techniques, for example:

Velvet should always be pressed over a velvet board, which is a board with closely spaced spikes all over it to allow the pile of the velvet to rest in them without being flattened. If you cannot get hold of a proper velvet board, it is a much better idea to avoid pressing altogether and just steam the garment. Boil a kettle and hold each piece of the garment in front of it, moving it to and fro to get the effect of pressing.

Lace: press on the wrong side over a thick towel, and use a moderately hot iron with a damp cloth.

Stretch fabrics: press very lightly on the wrong side over a damp cloth with a warm iron, taking care not to pull the fabric out of shape.

After pressing garments made from a fabric with a deep pile or nap (on the wrong side over a very slightly damp cloth), brush the right side of the garment to raise the pile again.

Another way is to stand the iron on its end and drape a wet cloth over its face. Draw the seam allowances across this, allowing the steam to come through the fabric.

Silks and woollens: should be pressed on the wrong side with a moderately hot iron but, whereas moisture should never be used with silk as it will leave water marks, it is usually required for woollens.

To remove shiny marks from fabrics, place the garment on the ironing board, right side up and cover it with a damp cloth. Press very quickly indeed with a hot iron and whip up the cloth. Turn the garment over and press on the wrong side of the fabric with a soft brush on heavy materials, and with a piece of soft dry cloth like muslin on lighter fabrics.

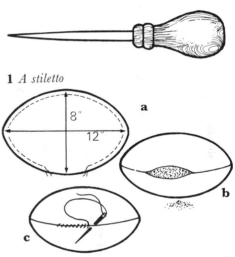

1 *A stiletto*

2 *Making a tailor's ham*

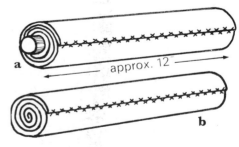

3 *Pressing roll*

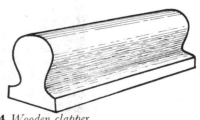

4 *Wooden clapper*

Tailoring

Step one

Introduction

A beautifully tailored garment is a pleasure to wear it sits well on the figure and fits the individual, perfectly, making you not only look good but feel good too.

Yet, despite its reputation to the contrary, tailoring is not difficult and with a little care and patience the results are great. You may well find it easier to make a successful and professional looking coat than a dress and will be surprised at how few people guess you have made it yourself. In addition you can save a great deal of money and will have a garment uniquely yours.

A tailored garment should have a fresh look, appearing as though little work and even less handling has been done. Many processes in fact, have, their parallel in dressmaking but techniques differ to accomodate the bulk in a coat-weight fabric. A perfect finish can only be achieved by means of accuracy, attention to detail, pressing, moulding and by fine hand stitching.

At the end of this section you will be able to attempt any coat pattern you wish. Each chapter takes you a step further in the construction of a coat, dealing with various alternatives rather than a separate complete coat in each chapter. For instance, in one chapter the coat is cut out, in another it is fitted and, when it comes to collars, cuffs and belts the different styles are covered in detail.

Coat fabrics

The fabric chosen for making a coat should be as good a quality as possible and not too heavy in weight. The weave should be close and firm, as the looser weaves tend to fray, causing difficulties during construction.

An ideal fabric is a 100% wool cloth made from short wool fibres which are processed to lie over each other in all directions. This produces a soft dense cloth with a slightly rough look as found in tweeds and flannels.

Equally good is a 100% wool worsted cloth made from long wool fibres which are processed to lie parallel to each other, producing a smooth fabric, usually with a well defined weave as found in suitings, serge and gabardine.

These two are often combined to make some very attractive fabrics.

It is best to avoid those fabrics with a large proportion of man made fibres as they do not always respond well to the techniques of pressing.

Fabric designs

There are many designs to choose from—herringbone, small checks, self coloured and tweeds being just a few from the large range available. It is wise to avoid large patterns and checks as these cause matching problems and some wastage of fabric.

Linings

The lining should complement the coat fabric in weight so it is often safer to buy both at once.

Satin forms a smooth, soft and shiny lining and is good for all weights of cloth but avoid buying a cheap one as it will not wear well.

Jap silk is a thin and soft lining, good for light weight cloth, but expensive. Satin backed crepe (satin with a crepe finish) is suitable as a heavy weight lining for tweeds. Milium is a satin weave backed with aluminium for warmth and useful for lining winter coats.

Interlinings

An interlining is used to give body to a light fabric or a loose weave, and to prevent creasing. It is tacked to the back of the main fabric and interlining and fabric are then made up as one.

Mull, a light woven cotton, cotton (not nylon) Organdie and Silesia are all suitable for use as interlinings.

Interfacings

An interfacing gives body to, and helps retain the shape of, a garment. It is placed between the fabric and the lining.

There are two groups of fabric used for interfacing:

Mixed fibre hair canvasses: can be used for all fabrics. Wool and hair is the best mixture for keeping shapes moulded into it. It is very springy and is crease resistant whereas the cotton and hair mixture is slightly springy but has the disadvantage of creasing easily.

Single fibre interfacings: Pure wool is very springy and soft and is useful for the light-weight tweeds. Linen canvas is very soft and will maintain a crease. It is used with very light cloths and as a backing for pockets. French canvas is made with the warp and weft threads of equal weight and will give a firm control to the under collar.

Padding

Tailor's wadding: used for making shoulder pads and padding sleeve heads.

Felt or domette: these are used for light padding at chest or back to give shaping without weight.

Patterns and notions

Paper patterns: When choosing a style look for one which has clean, uncluttered lines. The pattern should be fashionable but not so extreme as to be unwearable in six month's time. As it is not to easy to mould the end of a wide bust dart, choose a pattern with a seam over the bust or one with side front seams and a small bust dart.

Buy your usual size pattern as any extra ease needed will have been allowed for by the designer already.

Stay tape: 1.3m ($\frac{1}{2}$in) wide linen tape for holding the front seams of coats.

Threads: a variety are used in tailoring. Silk is used for all hand stitching and mercerised cotton for all machine stitching. Use a 50 for light to medium weight fabrics and 40 for heavy weight fabric. Silk buttonhole twist should be used for handworked buttonholes.

A gimp will also be necessary for buttonholes but if difficult to obtain two layers of buttonhole twist can be substituted.

Buttons: the choice is very wide, but be sure to choose ones which will suit the coat style: plain for a country tweed, self fabric for a town coat, leather for a car coat, silver or gilt for a blazer.

Good haberdashers will make buttons from your own fabric and if you wish will incorporate leather, silver or gilt for an individual touch.

Preparing the fabric

To prevent press marks which may occur on woollen fabrics it is advisable to steam press the length before cutting out.

Unfold the fabric and lay it right side down on a clean blanket, preferably on the floor to avoid creasing.

Steam press all over, lifting the iron each time. Do not push the iron as this tends to distort the grain. Cover the fabric with a thoroughly dampend cloth and press with an iron hot enough to hiss as it touches the cloth. Hang the cloth to dry.

Cutting out

Trim the paper pattern to the cutting line. Following the instruction sheet layout, place the pattern pieces on the fabric. To make sure the grain lines are correct, measure out equal distances from the selvedge to each end of the arrow on the pattern. Smooth the paper and pin every 5cm (2in) along the stitching line. Cut out carefully. It is wise to make seam allowances of 2.5cm (1in) at shoulders, armholes and side seams to allow for alterations.

Marking the fabric

With pieces laid flat transfer pattern markings to the fabric using tailor's tacks and thread markings. Chalk and tracing paper lines are not permanent enough for tailoring, as accuracy is essential for a perfect fit.

After cutting out and before removing the paper pattern, mark all stitching lines with continuous tailor's tacks. To do so, thread a needle with double thread and, on the stitching line, make stitches through both layers of fabric and the pattern, a loop being made at each stitch.

To remove the pattern, snip through the centre of each loop, unpin the pattern and gently ease the paper away. Gently pull the fabric edges apart and cut the stitches, leaving tufts on both sides. Mark the wrong sides of each piece with a chalk cross.

For marking balance marks and style details, use single tailor's tacks. With double thread take a stitch through the dot or hole in the pattern and both layers of fabric. Repeat leaving a loop. Snip the loop before removing the pattern.

Thread marking is used for marking centre back, centre front and alteration and style lines. Work a continuous line of stitches through one layer of fabric. If a colour code routine is adopted in this marking it saves confusion later—

Right. *A beautifully fitted wrap around coat with tie belt from the Butterick range, pattern* 9005, *made up in a striking check fabric with trousers made to match.*

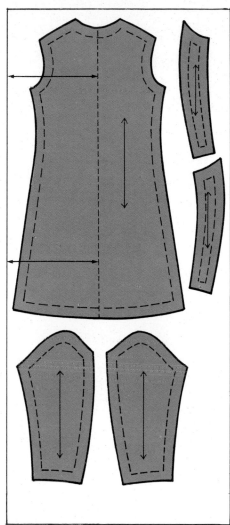

1 Coat pieces tacked to interlining

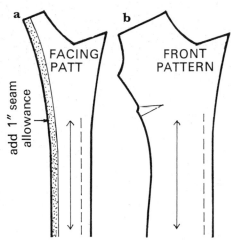

2 Centre front interfacing: **a** using facing pattern; **b** using front pattern

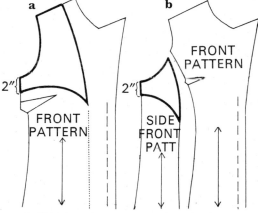

3 Side front interfacing, **a** for front without side front seams; **b** for front with side front seam

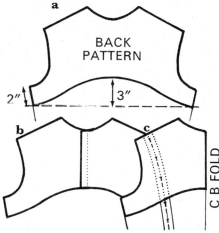

4 Back interfacing; **a** for back without seams; **b** for back with centre back seams; **c** for back with side back seams

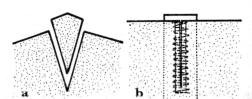

5 Interfacing darts: **a** cutting out dart **b** stitching dart together on stay tape

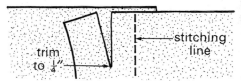

6 Stitching interfacing seams

so tailor's tack seam lines in white and use colours for matching balance points.

Inter or underlining

If it is necessary to interline the fabric work as follows:

After the coat fabric has been cut out, marked up and separated, place each back front and sleeve piece on to the single interlining fabric. Place the wrong side to the interlining, matching the grain. Tack all round 2.5cm (1in) in from the stitching line (Fig. 1). Cut out and work interlining and coat fabric as one.

Interfacing

All tailored coats should have an interfacing. The interfacing should be steam pressed before cutting out to prevent shrinkage during shaping.

Coat and interfacing grains should coincide to avoid the possibility of distortion.

For each front, cut one piece of canvas as for the facing, adding an extra 2.5cm (1in) seam allowance at the inner edge (Fig. 2a). If your pattern has a side front seam use the front pattern complete instead of the facing pattern (Fig. 2b). Cut a second piece of inter facing for each front to include the armhole, using the front, or side front, pattern as a guide (Fig. 3a and b).

For the back, cut canvas to include the neck and armhole, using the back pattern as a guide and curving the lower edge (Fig. 4a). If there is a centre back seam cut two pieces of canvas and join them at the centre back (Fig. 4b). Where you have side back seams, overlap the pattern pieces on the stitching line and cut (Fig. 4c).

Darts and seams

There are two ways to give shaping to the canvas interfacings, but you must fit the tacked canvas and coat before shaping.

For darts, cut the dart shape out along the stitching line. Place the cut edges together over the stay tape and machine stitch (Fig. 5a and b).

For the seams, overlay on the stitching line, machine stitch and then trim the seam allowances to 0.6cm (¼in) (Fig. 6). Press the canvas over a tailor's ham to retain its shape.

Herringbone stitch

Step two

Basting

Basting is usually worked on seams, details and canvasses to ensure that the grain is kept correctly aligned and is not pulled out of shape whilst being worked. Always work on a flat surface.

Seams and details

Lay the pattern pieces flat, right sides together, notches and balance marks matching exactly. Pin at right angles to the stitching line (Fig. 1) and baste.

Seams with ease

On some patterns shaping is obtained not by a dart but by easing one seam to another.

Lay the pieces together, right sides facing, with the one to be eased on top. Pin the notches and divide ease equally along the length (Fig. 2a). Push ease down with fingers and baste, taking a small section at a time (Fig. 2b).

Back shoulder dart

In most cases it is better to ease in the back shoulder dart for a smoother line rather than stitch the dart. Exceptions are with linen, or fabric with a high man-made fibre content, because it is not so easy to shrink these fibres.

Overbasting

Overbasting is used when basting for a fitting to give a smooth line and a better indication of fit (Fig. 3).

The first fitting
Preparation for the first fitting

Before any sewing is done the coat must be basted together. tried on to see that it fits, and initial alterations made. On the back, baste the style seams. Baste the canvas to the wrong side along the neck and armholes (Fig. 4a). On the front, baste the style seams and the canvas darts or seams, then baste the canvas to the wrong side (Fig. 4b). Also baste the sleeve seams.
Baste the centre back seam of the under-collar then the collar canvas to the wrong side of the under collar (Fig. 4c). Overbaste the side and shoulder seams and the under collar to the neck (Fig. 4d). Baste the sleeves to the coat taking great care to spread the ease evenly at the sleeve head.

Fitting points

A well fitted coat feels comfortable, adjusts naturally to the activities of the wearer, is becoming in line and amount of ease, and is consistent with the current fashion.
Five interrelated factors are to be looked for when fitting a coat:
Ease: there should be ease for movement without the coat being too large.
Line: all vertical seams should be at right angles to the ground unless they are fashion features designed to be otherwise. All horizontal lines—the bust, waist, hips—should be at right angles to the vertical lines.
Grain: as for line.
Set or Fit: a garment which sets well sits on the figure without wrinkles or strain.
Balance: pockets, belts, buttons, hems to be proportioned correctly for the individual figure.

Correcting the faults

Put on the coat, right side out, over the appropriate clothing. Pin the centre front lines together and then check the following points. It is better if you can get a friend to help you.
Is the coat sitting on the figure correctly (Fig. 5)? Are the lower edges level, the centre back and centre front lines vertical? Are the style lines right for the figure—sometimes a line over the bust can be moved for better balance (Fig. 6).
Look for strain points shown by wrinkles (Fig. 7a). Unbaste and let seams out until wrinkles have gone. Re-pin. If the coat is too big it will hang in folds (Fig. 7b). Unbaste and repin.
Turn up the hem and check buttonhole and pocket positions. Unless they are fashion features, pockets should be placed so that they are easy to use— the usual position is about 5cm (2in) below the waist and between the centre front and side seam. If your hip or stomach is rather large a pocket could be inserted in a seam to give a smoother line.
Check that the fold of the lapel is lying smoothly and continues on the under-collar (Fig. 8a and b). An adjustment to the top button position can correct a loose or tight neck line (Fig. 8c). An adjustment at the back neck seam may be necessary for a shawl collar to sit well. Pin along the folds and thread mark when unbasted (Fig. 8a and b).
See that the sleeve hangs smoothly, that it is not too large or tight, and that the armhole line is well balanced. However, no alterations to the sleeve are made at this stage; the sleeves are put in to check the appearance and balance of the coat.

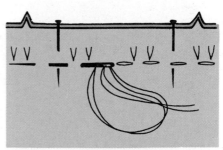

1 *Basting a straight seam*

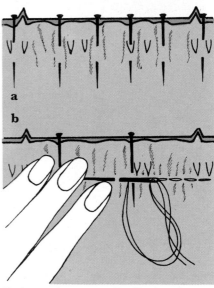

2 *An eased seam:* **a** *distributing the ease;* **b** *pushing in the ease and basting*

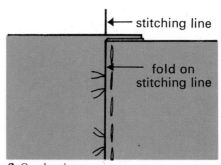

3 *Overbasting*

Pinning alterations

To let out or take in a seam, first un-baste. Find the correct position for the seam then fold one side on the new stitching line and pin fold to new stitching line on under piece (Fig. 9a and b).

Marking alterations

On shoulders and side seams thread mark any alterations in a new coloured thread. Mark through the fold and along the under piece (Fig. 10). Re-

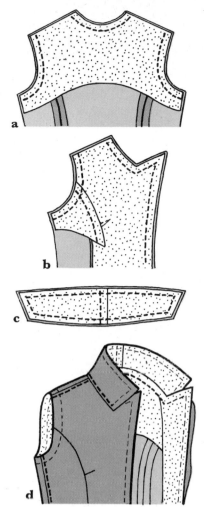

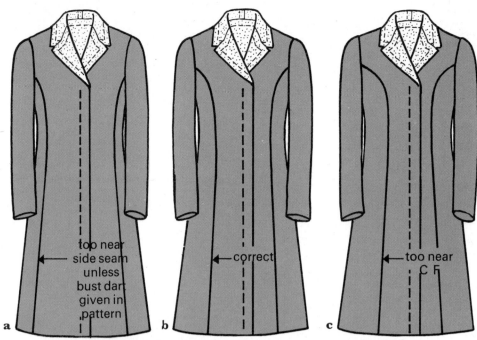

6 *Checking the position of the style lines over the bust*

too near side seam unless bust dart given in pattern

a

correct

b

too near C F

c

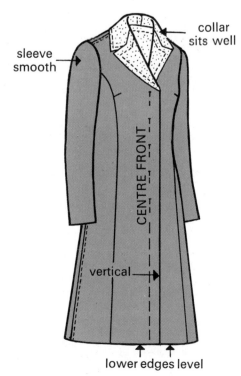

4 *Preparing for first fitting:* **a** *back;* **b** *front;* **c** *under collar;* **d** *overbasting shoulder, side and neck seams.*

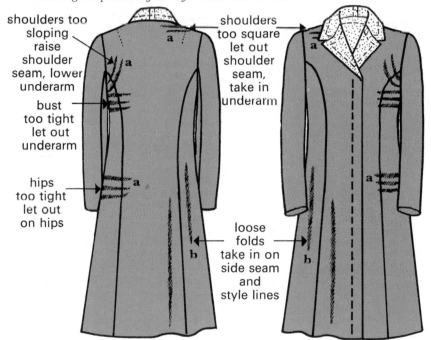

shoulders too sloping raise shoulder seam, lower underarm

bust too tight let out underarm

hips too tight let out on hips

shoulders too square let out shoulder seam, take in underarm

loose folds take in on side seam and style lines

a

b

7 *Fitting points to watch out for:* **a** *usual strain points;* **b** *loose folds*

collar sits well

sleeve smooth

CENTRE FRONT

vertical

lower edges level

5 *Checking the lines of the coat*

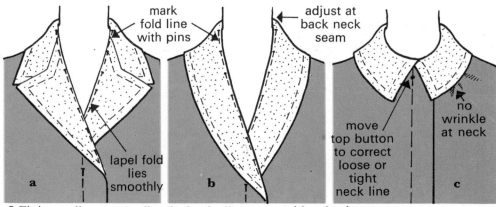

mark fold line with pins

lapel fold lies smoothly

a

adjust at back neck seam

b

move top button to correct loose or tight neck line

no wrinkle at neck

c

8 *Fitting a collar:* **a** *step collar;* **b** *shawl collar;* **c** *coat without lapels*

move old markings. On style seams slip baste any alterations (Fig.11) by folding the top piece under on the sewing line and place the fold over the sewing line of the lower piecc. Sew taking a 1cm (½in) stitch through the fold then a 1cm (½in) stitch through under piece along the sewing line. Remove old markings.

Preparing to stitch
Unbaste sleeve, undercollar, shoulder and side seams, but leave the style seams basted.

Seams
To avoid damage to the fabric remove the tailor's tacks before machining and then stitch just outside the line of basting without catching it (Fig. 12). Seams with ease should be stitched with the ease side up as they are easier to control this way.

Shoulder seams are best hand sewn. For a firm result use a double silk thread and a back stitch (Fig. 13). By doing this the ease is controlled, resulting in a straight line. Before a seam is pressed the basting is removed and the edges neatened by overcasting in matching silk thread (Fig. 14).

Topstitching
Topstitching gives a professional finish when done carefully, so practise on a piece of fabric folded to the appropriate thickness. Work the topstitching as the garment is being made, not when it is finished.

Set the machine to a large stitch and use a number 16 (or 100) needle. If possible use buttonhole twist in both bottom and top of the machine. If this does not work try threading the top only.

Baste just inside the topstitching line (Fig. 15). Then stitch slowly and carefully, using basting, seam and machine foot as guide lines. When turning corners leave the needle in the work and pivot cloth on the needle.

Pressing
To ensure a smoothly finished garment each stage of the work should be pressed as it is finished. This needs care and plenty of patience. Remember that pressing is not ironing and that the iron should be lifted and pressed upon the part required—not smoothed to and fro.

The positioning of the garment or part to be pressed is important and you should always work in the direction of the grain. (Fig. 16) Always test for the correct iron temperature on a spare piece of fabric. If there are any arti-

ficial fibres in the cloth regulate the heat to these to avoid destroying them. Pressing cloths must be damp rather than wet to avoid spoiling the appearance of the fabric and leaving a rough-dry look. As the iron is lifted after each pressing, quickly remove the damp cloth and hold the tailor's clapper firmly over the pressed section for some seconds (Fig. 17). This action helps to set the seam or edge professionally, ensuring a crisper fold or flatter surface. Press and clap the folds of pleats, hems, seams, darts, pockets and edges as the construction of the garment proceeds.

Pressing seams
Remove all basting and press the seam flat to blend the stitches. Lay the seam over a pressing roll, making sure that the rest of the garment is well supported. Press open with the point of an iron (Fig. 19). Look at the right side to make sure the seam line is flat before pressing with a damp cloth and clapping heavily on the wrong side (Fig. 20).

Pressing eased seams
Where a seam has been eased or fabric is to be moulded the technique of shrinking is used.

Lay the garment flat on an ironing board, right side down. Shrink away the ease with the point of the iron and a damp pressing cloth (Fig. 21). Open the seam, lay over a pressing roll and shrink the eased seam edge. While damp stretch the uneased edge to make it lie flat as in curved seams (Fig. 22). Finally press and clap the seam.

Pressing darts
After stitching, cut along the fold of the dart, cutting as near to the point as possible (Fig. 23a). Lay the dart right side down over a ham (Fig. 23b) and press and clap the dart open, checking for a smooth line.

Top pressing
Top pressing is used for lapels, collars and the final press.

Lay the garment on an ironing board right side up, smoothed into the correct position with the grain undistorted. Cover with a piece of light-weight wool cloth. Over this place the pressing cloth and press lightly. This prevents shine and removes any pin, basting or seam marks which might have been accidentally pressed in.

Pleats
Because of the heavier fabrics used in tailoring all pleats need to be supported to prevent them dragging and upsetting the balance of the garment.

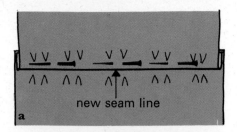
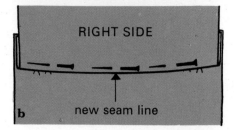
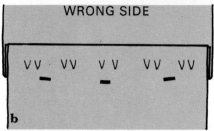

9a, b *Letting out and taking in a seam*

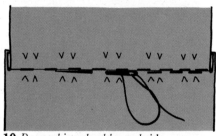

10 *Re-marking shoulder and side seams*

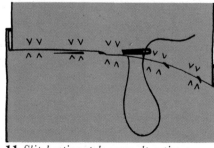

11 *Slip basting style seam alterations*

Inverted pleat
Baste, fit, stitch, snip and neaten the seams (Fig. 24a). Press open. Put seams in line and press pleat, placing brown paper or card under the fold to prevent marking the fabric. Cut a strip of lining to the pleat width plus 1.3cm (½in), and to the length from the top stitching line of the pleat to the neck or waist (Fig. 24b). Turn under each long edge for 0.6cm (¼in) and stitch.

Stitch this strip to each fold of the pleat (Fig. 24c). Fold up and stitch it to the coat just above the neck or waist seam. Trim to the curve (Fig. 24d).

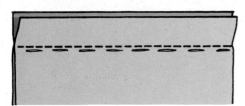

12 *Stitching just outside the basting*

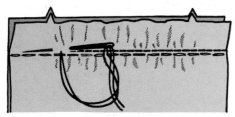

13 *Backstitching an eased shoulder seam*

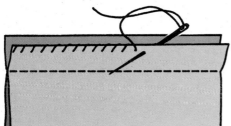

14 *Overcasting the seam edges*

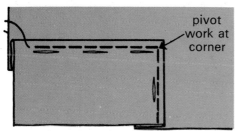

15 *Topstitching just outside the basting*

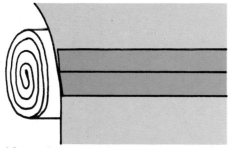

16 *Pressing a carefully positioned seam*

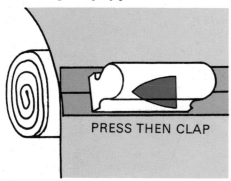

17 *Using a tailor's clapper*

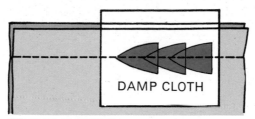

18 *A seam pressed flat*

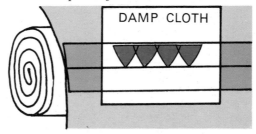

19 *Pressing a seam open with point of iron*

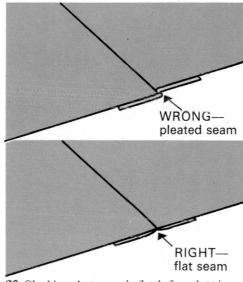

20 *Checking that seam is flat before clapping*

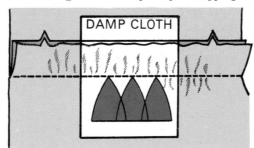

21 *Shrinking ease in a seam*

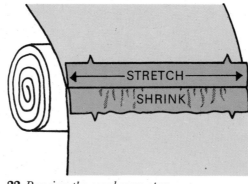

22 *Pressing the eased seam open*

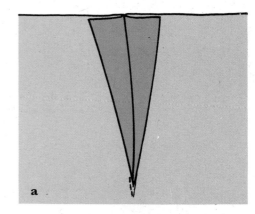

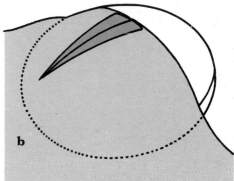

23 *Cutting a dart open;* **b** *positioning open dart over a tailor's ham*

Decorative topstitching

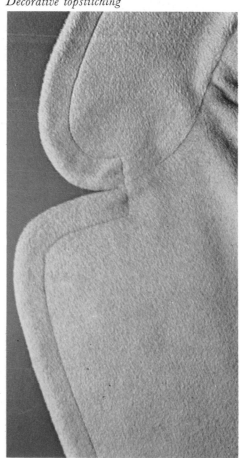

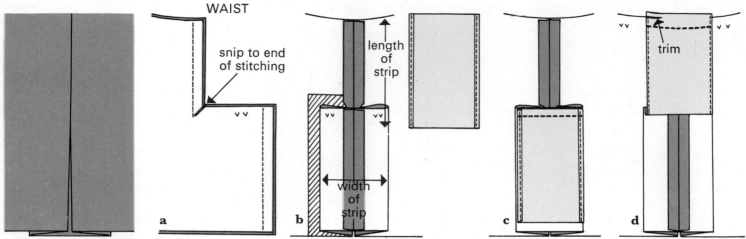

24 *Inverted pleat:* **a** *stitch, neaten and snip the seam;* **b** *press pleat and prepare lining strip;* **c** *lining stitched to top of pleat;* **d** *trimming top edge of lining strip*

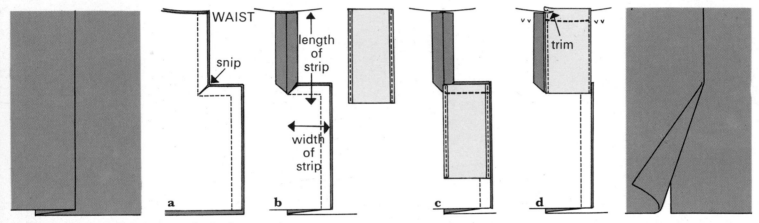

25 *Knife pleat:* **a** *stitch, neaten and snip the seam;* **b** *press seam and prepare lining strip;* **c** *lining stitched to top of pleat;* **d** *trimming top edge of lining*

26 *A back slit*

Knife pleat

Baste, fit, stitch, snip and neaten seams (Fig. 25a). Press the coat seam open and the pleat seam flat. Cut a strip of lining fabric to the pleat width plus 1.3cm (½in), and to the length from top stitching line of slit to the neck or waist (Fig. 25b). Turn under the long edges for 0.6cm (¼in) and stitch. Stitch this strip to the top of the pleat (Fig.25c). Fold up and stitch it to the coat just above the neck or waist seam (Fig. 25d). Trim to the curve.

Slit opening

Stitch as given for the slit opening in the pattern, then support as for a knife pleat (Fig.26).

Terms and stitches

Basting: firm tacking with 0.6cm (¼in) stitches.
Easing: instead of a dart, shaping is obtained by easing one seam to another.
Shrinking: to shrink away the extra fullness which gives ease and to create shaping.

Slip basting: used to baste a seam from the right side altering a seam (also used to match patterns, plaids, stripes etc). Fold top piece under on sewing line. Place fold over sewing line of lower piece. Sew taking a 1cm (½in) stitch through fold then a 1cm (½in) stitch through under piece along the sewing line.

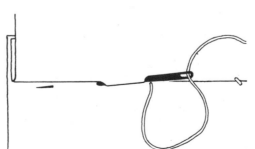

Stretching: to stretch fabric to make it lie flat as in curved seams, and to create shaping.
Tailor's knot:

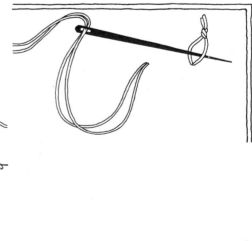

Step three

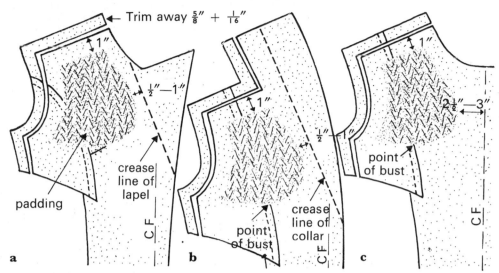

Trim away $\frac{5}{8}'' + \frac{1}{16}''$

padding

crease line of lapel

C F

point of bust

crease line of collar

C F

point of bust

C F

1 *Padding front canvas:* **a** *step collar;* **b** *shawl collar;* **c** *front without revers*

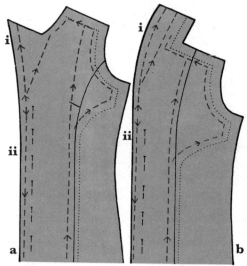

2 *Basting front canvas to coat;* **a** *step collar;* **b** *shawl collar*

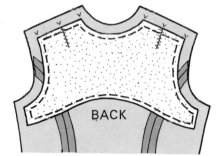

BACK

3 *Basting the back canvas to the coat*

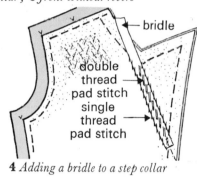

bridle

double thread pad stitch

single thread pad stitch

4 *Adding a bridle to a step collar*

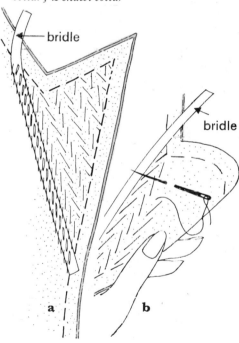

bridle

bridle

5a *and* **b** *Pad stitching the step collar*

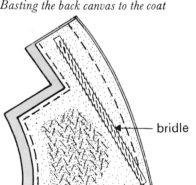

bridle

6 *Adding a bridle to a shawl collar*

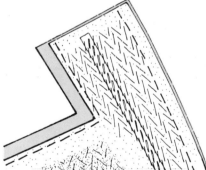

7 *Pad stitching the shawl collar*

Canvassing the front and back

The canvas is sewn in place after any style seams, darts and back seams have been stitched but before the shoulder seams and side seams are stitched.

Padding the front canvas

After stitching the darts or seams on the canvas, trim off the seam allowance plus 0.2cm ($\frac{1}{16}$in) on the underarm, armhole and shoulder to reduce bulk in the seams.

To give a rounded line to the chest add a chest pad of felt or domette to the side of the canvas which faces the lining using staggered rows of pad stitching (Fig. 1).

Basting canvas to the front

Lay the canvas flat on a table, padded side down and lay the corresponding coat front over it with the wrong side of the coat fabric facing the canvas. Match and pin the centre and crease lines together. Baste the following (Fig. 2a and b)

(i) Working from the bust line upwards, baste the front edges of the coat to the canvas, smoothing it up while working to prevent wrinkles.

(ii) Repeat from the bustline downwards.

(iii) Baste the opposite edge of the canvas in a line from the hem through the bust up to the shoulder.

(iv) Baste round the armhole and along the shoulder.

(v) Finally baste along the crease line of the lapel.

Basting canvas to the back

Trim off the seam allowance plus 0.2cm ($\frac{1}{16}$in) round underarm, armhole, shoulder and neck edges.

Stitch any darts or seams. Even if you have decided to dispense with the back shoulder dart and ease in the shoulder seam instead, the dart should be made on the canvas.

Baste the canvas to the wrong side of the coat back (Fig. 3), easing the coat fabric to the canvas along the back shoulder seam if necessary.

Adding a bridle
A bridle is a piece of 1.3cm (½in) wide linen tape sewn to the canvas along the roll line of a lapel, continuing into the step collar for 5cm (2in) or to the centre back for a shawl collar. The linen tape should be shrunk by damp pressing or washing before application to prevent more shrinkage later.

Step collar. Cut a piece of tape to the length of the crease line plus 5cm (2in) to extend into the collar.
Pin the tape centrally along the crease line with 5cm (2in) extending at the neck edge (Fig. 4). Keep the tape taut. Using a double, matching silk thread pad stitch the tape in place along the centre line. Then, with a single silk thread, pad stitch along each edge. Starting from the bridle work rows of staggered pad stitching towards the edge. Keep the rows in line with the edge (Fig. 5a and b). Keep the rows in line with the bridle and don't sew beyond the seam line. Hold the lapel in a curled position with the left hand.
Shawl collar. Cut a piece of tape to the length of the crease line. Pin tape centrally along the crease line keeping it taut (Fig.6). Using a double matching silk thread, pad stitch the tape in place along the centre. Then, with single thread, pad stitch the tape in place along each edge.
Starting from the bridle, work rows of pad stitching towards the edge (Fig. 7). Shape the rows slightly at the outer edge to allow the collar to set correctly, and don't sew beyond the seam line. While working, roll the collar in a curled position with the left hand as for the step collar (Fig. 5b).

Front stay tape
Stay tape is sewn to the front edges. On a coat with a step collar the tape extends from the hem to the top of the crease line (Fig. 8a) and on a coat with a shawl collar from hem to centre back (Fig. 8b). On any other style the tape is taken up the front to the neck edge (Fig. 8c)
Before adding the stay tape, trim the front edge of the canvas just within the sewing line to reduce bulk (Fig. 9). Cut linen tape to the required length and position the tape and baste the strip taut at the outer edge. Catch stitch the inner edge to the canvas.

Finishing the canvassing
Finally, catch stitch the canvas to the coat at the underarm, shoulder and armhole on both back and front.

Take care not to pull the stitches tight. Working on the wrong side press well up to the crease line. Fold back along the crease line and allow the collar to roll, but do not press.

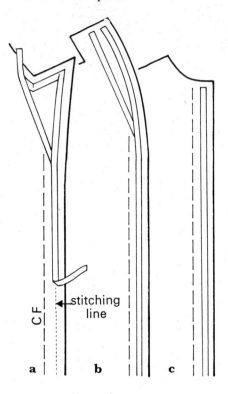

8 *Stay tape stitched to front of coat with;* **a** *step collar;* **b** *shawl collar;* **c** *coat without revers*

Piped buttonholes
There are several ways of making fabric buttonholes. For the heavier weight fabrics used in tailoring the following method is very successful.

Marking the buttonholes
The buttonhole length is the diameter of the button plus 0.3cm (⅛in). If you are not buying the size of button suggested in the pattern then re-mark moving the outside tailor's tacks.
To ensure that the buttonholes are in line and parallel to each other, prepare tram-lines on the markings, tacking through both fabric and canvas (Fig. 10). Remove the tailor's tacks.

Making the buttonholes
For each buttonhole cut two pipes in the coat fabric. The pipes should be 2.5cm (1in) wide and the length of the buttonhole plus 4cm (1½in), cut in the straight grain of the fabric.
Position the pipes on the right side of the garment, with the edges meeting along the buttonhole line and right sides facing (Fig. 11) then baste. Chalk mark the ends of the buttonhole. Working on the right side, stitch along the buttonhole length to each side of the

buttonhole marking (Fig. 12). The lines should be 0.6cm (¼in) apart for buttonholes and 1.3cm (½in) apart for pockets. At each end of the stitching over stitch for about 1.3cm (½in).
Remove the tram-lines then working on the wrong side, cut along the buttonhole line making deep mitred 'V's at the corners at least 1cm (⅜in) deep (Fig. 13). Take care not to cut the pipes. Pull the pipes through the opening to the wrong side (Fig. 14). Press the seams open, and the mitres away from the buttonhole.
Working on the right side adjust the pipes into even folds and oversew to close (Fig. 15). Stab stitch along the seamline.
At the back work an oversewing stitch at each end of the buttonhole to hold the facing in position (Fig. 16). Fold garment back and back stitch through pipes and mitre as near to the fold as possible (Fig. 17).

Pockets with lining
Pockets can be functional or decorative. The right place for them varies for each figure so make sure at the first fitting that they are in the right position for you.

Interfacing a pocket
All pocket openings are interfaced with a strip of silesia, or duck, basted on the wrong side of the opening to support them. Cut the interfacing with the grain falling along the line of the pocket where possible, and take it into a seam where practicable (Fig. 18). Position and baste to the wrong side of the pocket opening, then make up the pocket as follows.

Straight piped pocket
This type of pocket looks well if made with contrast pipes (Fig. 19). The average pocket length for a coat is 14cm (5½in) to 15.2cm (6in). For each pocket cut two pipes 5cm (2in) wide and to the pocket length plus 4cm (1½in), in the straight grain of the fabric. Make the pocket opening as for bound buttonholes, but with the stitching lines 1.3cm (½in) apart. To finish, add the pocket backing and lining as shown below.

Shaped piped pocket.
Mark pocket position carefully with basting then interface the back. To pipe the pocket cut a piece of fabric suitable for the pocket shape, using coat or contrast fabric (Fig. 21). Position the piece of material, right sides facing, over the marked pocket opening, matching any design or check if appropriate. Baste in place along

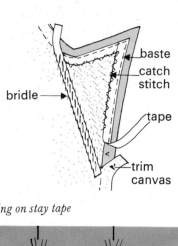

9 *Sewing on stay tape*

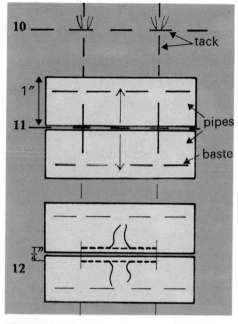

10-17 *Making a piped buttonhole*

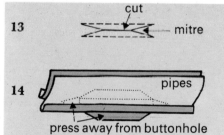

13

14

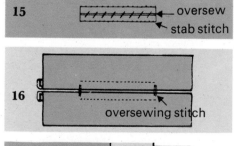

15

16

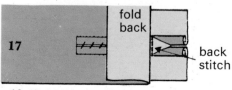

17

18 *Cutting the pocket interfacing*

19 *Straight piped pocket*

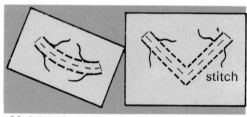

20 *Shaped piped pocket*

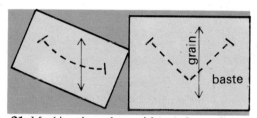

21 *Marking the pocket position on the patch*

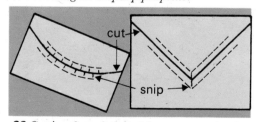

22 *Stitching the shaped piped pocket*

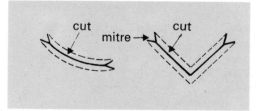

23 *Cutting through the patch*

24 *Cutting the coat along the pocket opening*

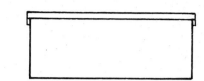

25 *A piped flap pocket*

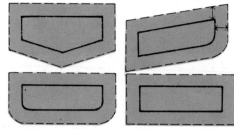

26 *Cutting various pocket flaps*

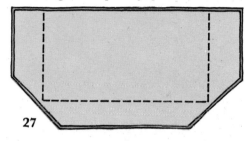

27

28

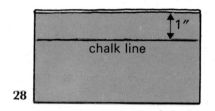

29

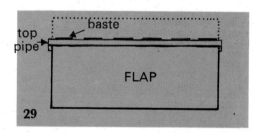

30

27-30 *Making the pocket flap*

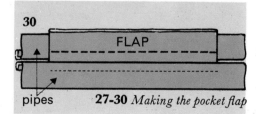

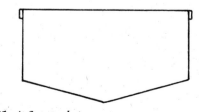

31 *A flap pocket*

75

pocket line.
Stitch carefully at equal distances from the basting (Fig. 22). The width depends on how you would like the pocket to look. Cut through the patch only (Fig. 23) then cut through the garment along the pocket opening (Fig. 24) mitring the corners. Finish as for a straight piped pocket, snipping any curved seams. Finally, add the pocket lining and backing.

Piped flap pocket

Make a piped pocket without lining. From the coat fabric cut a pocket flap to the length of the finished pocket and to the desired shape of flap, plus 2.5cm (1in) on all edges for seam allowance (Fig. 26). Cut a lining for the flap to match.
Place pieces together, right sides facing, and stitch (Fig. 27). Snip across corners. Turn to the right side and press, then draw a chalk line 2.5cm (1in) from the raw edge (Fig. 28). Slip the flap under the top pipe and baste in place through all layers along the stitching line of the top pipe (Fig. 29). Turn to the wrong side and stitch in place over the original seam at the back of the top pipe (Fig. 30).
To finish, add the pocket backing and lining.

Flap pocket

Make up the flap as for a piped flap pocket and cut one pipe as for a straight piped pocket.
Interface the wrong side of the pocket opening. Stitch the flap in place along the marked pocket opening, with right side facing (Fig. 32).
Fold the flap seam up, out of the way, and stitch the bottom pipe in place as for a piped buttonhole. Cut through the back of the opening as for a piped buttonhole (Fig. 33).
Turn the flap seam allowance through the opening to the wrong side, leaving the flap on the right side (Fig. 34). Press the flap seam allowance up and the mitres away from the opening. Pipe the lower seam opening as for a piped buttonhole (Fig. 35) and finish by adding the pocket backing and lining.

False flap pocket

Make a flap as for a piped flap pocket. Position over opening and stitch (Fig. 37). Cut away the corners and neaten the raw edge. Press the flap down and fasten the sides carefully (Fig. 38).

Welt pocket

Make up the welt as for the flap in Figs. 26, 27 and 28. Then make up as

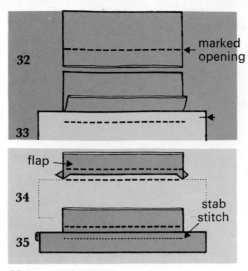

32–35 *Making the flap pocket*

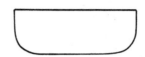

36 *A false flap pocket*

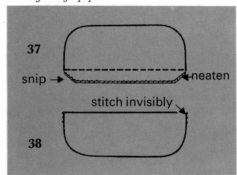

37–38 *Stitching the false flap pocket*

for a flap pocket but placing the welt to the lower edge and piping the top edge. Finish the backing and lining and press the welt up (Fig. 40). Stab stitch in place.
If the coat is finished with top stitching, top stitch the sides instead of stab stitching.

Lining a pocket

Cut a backing for the pocket in coat fabric, 9cm (3in) deep and to the length of the pipe. Stitch to the top pipe or flap seam allowance as near as possible to the original stitching line (Fig. 41). For added strength stitch again 1.3cm (½in) above the first row.
For each pocket cut two pieces of lining fabric 10cm (4in) deep and to the length of the pipe. Stitch one piece of lining to the lower edge of the backing and the other piece to the bottom pipe or welt seam allowance (Fig. 42). Round off the lower edges of the lining as shown then stitch round to make the pocket. Working on the right side stab stitch parallel to the mitre folds for added strength (Fig. 43).

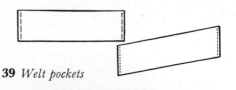

39 *Welt pockets*

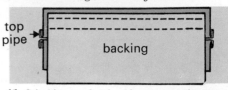

40 *Stab stitching the sides of the welt*

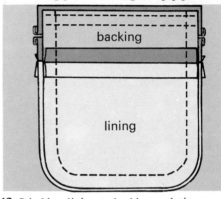

41 *Stitching pocket backing to top pipe*

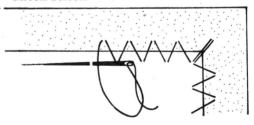

42 *Stitching lining to backing and pipe*

43 *Stab stitching parallel to mitre folds*

Terms and stitches
Catch stitch

Pad stitching

Stab stitch

Step four

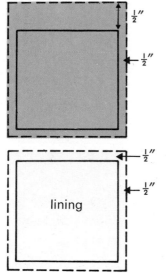

1 *Cutting out a patch pocket;* **a** *coat fabric* **b** *lining*

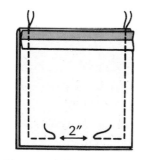

2 *Stitching lining to pocket along the top*

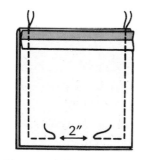

3 *Stitching round the pocket*

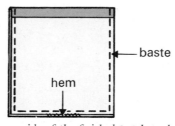

4 *The wrong side of the finished patch pocket*

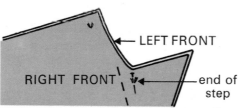

5 *Sewing the pocket to the coat:* **a** *with machine to stitching;* **b** *with ladder stitch*

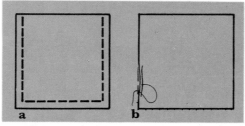

6 *Marking ends of the steps on a step collar*

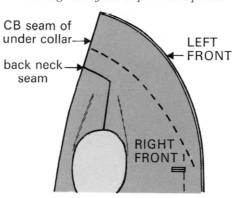

7 *Checking that both lapels on a shawl collar are the same*

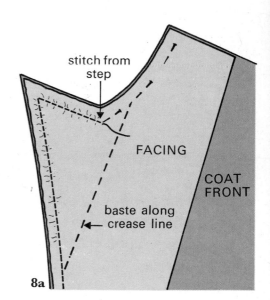

8a

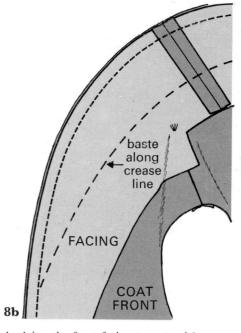

8b

8 *Applying the front facing to coat with* **a** *step collar;* **b** *shawl collar*

Patch pockets

Cut out the pocket shape with 1.3cm (½in) seam allowance all round plus an extra 2.5cm (1in) along the top edge (Fig. 1). Then cut out the lining 2.5cm (1in) shorter than the pocket. Stitch the lining to the pocket along the top, taking 1.3cm (½in) seam (Fig. 2). Press the seam open.
Fold lining to the pocket, right sides facing. Stitch, leaving a 5cm (2in) opening at the lower edge (Fig. 3). Snip curved seams if any or snip across corners. Turn through the opening, baste flat round edges and hem open-ing to close (Fig. 4). Press and clap. Apply to coat by topstitching (Fig. 5a) or ladder stitch (Fig. 5b). If this is not secure enough backstitch the pocket in place, working from the wrong side of the coat.

Facing the coat front
Coat with lapels

If working on a step collar mark the steps on the top edges of the lapels so they are both the same (Fig. 6). If working on a shawl collar, stitch and press the centre back seam of the under-collar, then stitch the shoulder and back neck seams. Press open and clap. Fold the coat in half and check that both sides have the same curve (Fig. 7).
Lay the facing and coat right sides together. Baste with small stitches to control the slight fullness there may be on the facing of the lapels (Fig. 8a and b). Baste along the crease line. Stitch carefully as given on the instruction sheet, taking care to keep both lapels the same. Note that the step collar is only stitched as far as the end of the step.
Remove basting. Snip across corners, snip into the end of the stitching line if

applicable, and layer the seam allowances (Fig. 9a and b). Press the seam over a pressing roll.

Turn the facing to the inside. Working on the underside of the lapel baste the same edge of the lapel so that it lies away from the top edge and baste along the crease line (Fig. 10a and b). Baste the remainder of the facing seam to lie away from the top of the coat. To press the lapel lay it flat, right side down, on an ironing board. Cover with a damp cloth and press as far as the crease line and clap. Press and clap the rest of the front edge.

Lay the coat right side up with lapel folded in position and lightly press over a ham, using a woollen cloth under the pressing cloth. Press the wrong side of the lower coat on a flat board. Side stitch under the lapel and down the inside front to keep the seam in position (Fig. 11a and b).

Coat without lapels

Apply the facing as given on your pattern instruction sheet and follow the steps given above for coats with lapels, ignoring those points referring specifically to the lapels. The whole of the front seam edge should be basted to lie towards the inside of the coat and then side stitched (Fig. 12).

Belts

You can add your own belt to a plain coat to give back interest. The belt can be set into the side seams and go right across the back, (Fig. 13a) set into the side seams and sewn or buttoned at the side back (Fig. 13b) or it can be set across the centre back (Fig. 13c). You can also have a tie belt (Fig. 13d) or a bukled belt (Fig. 13e).

For all belts you will need two pieces of the coat fabric each to the required width plus 1.3cm (½in) seam allowance all round and one piece of interfacing to the same measurements (Fig. 14).

If you are making buttonholes, baste the interfacing to the wrong side of one belt piece and make the buttonhole (Fig. 15). Place the belt pieces together, right sides facing, and lay the interfacing on the top. Baste together (Fig. 16).

Belt across back

Stitch the long edges, layer the seam allowances, turn, baste and press (Fig. 17). Topstitch to match coat if required (Fig. 18). When fitting make sure the belt is correctly balanced for the figure, usually above the waist for a short figure and below the waist for a tall figure (Fig. 19).

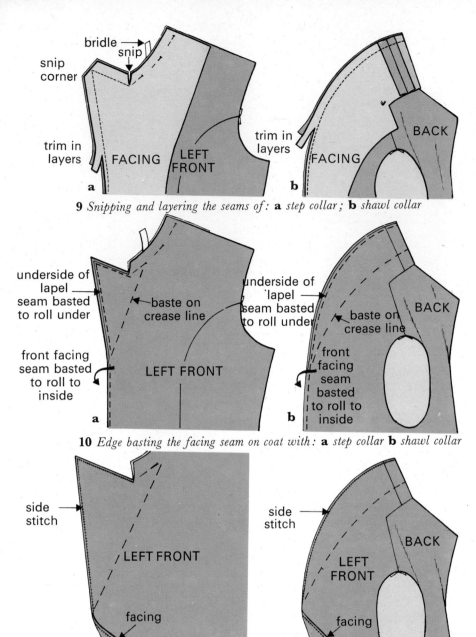

9 *Snipping and layering the seams of:* **a** *step collar;* **b** *shawl collar*

10 *Edge basting the facing seam on coat with:* **a** *step collar* **b** *shawl collar*

11 *Facing seam side stitched under lapels and down front:* **a** *step collar;* **b** *shawl collar*

Quarter belt at side seams

Make the buttonholes and shape the end (Fig. 20). Stitch long edges and across shaped end. Snip and layer the seam allowances, turn baste and press (Fig. 21). Topstitch if required. When fitting make sure that both belts are balanced and the same length. The belt should be just above the waist for a short figure (Fig. 22a) and just below the waist for a tall figure (Fig. 22b).

Half belt at back

Make the buttonholes and shape ends (Fig. 23). Stitch the belt all round leaving a 5cm to 10cm (2in to 4in) opening along one side. Snip and layer the seam allowances, turn, baste and press (Fig. 24). Hem opening to close. Topstitch if required. When fitting check for balance as for the belt across the back.

Tie belt

Should be made up as for the half belt across the back (Fig. 25).

Belt with buckle

Make up as for ¼ belt. Fold unstitched end through buckle. Turn under raw ends and herringbone (Fig. 26).

The second fitting

Having made the coat fronts, belt (if required) and stitched the back seams, it is now time for the second fitting.

Preparing for the fitting

Working on the new fitting lines, baste the side seams. Baste the shoulder seams if not already sewn. Over baste the under collar. Sew a running thread between the notches on the sleeve heads to help distribute the ease (Fig.

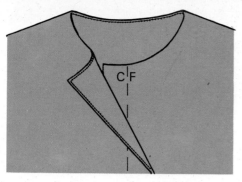

12 *Side stitching coat without lapels*

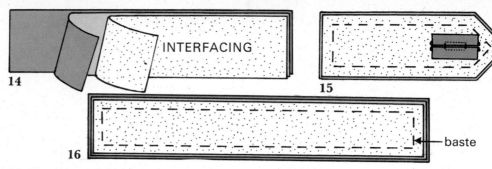

14 *The pieces needed to make up a belt* **15** *Making bound buttonholes on a belt* **16** *The pieces basted and ready for stitching*

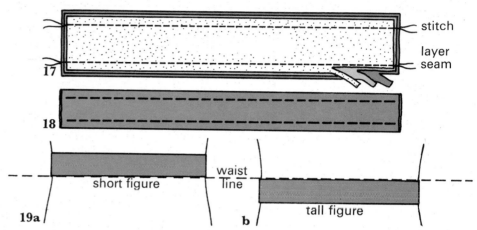

17 *The belt across back stitched and ready for turning* **18** *Topstitching the belt across back*
19 *Positioning belt across back;* **a** *above waist on short figure;* **b** *below waist on tall figure*

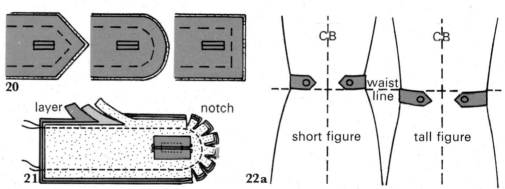

20 *Shaping the end of a ¼ belt at side seam* **21** *Stitching the ¼ belt* **22** *Positioning a ¼ belt on:* **a** *a short figure;* **b** *a tall figure*

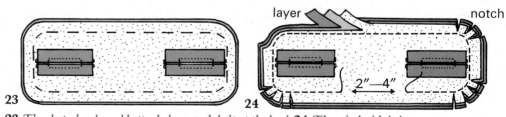

23 *The shaped ends and buttonholes on a ½ belt at the back* **24** *The stitched ½ belt.*

13 *Belts:* **a** *right across back;* **b** ¼ *belt buttoned at side back;* **c** ½ *belt at centre back;* **d** *tie belt;* **e** *buckle belt.*

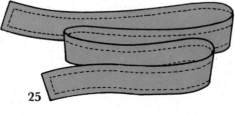

25 *A tie belt*

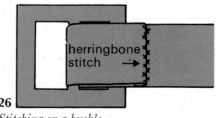

26 *Stitching on a buckle*

27 *Running a thread between the notches on the sleeve head*

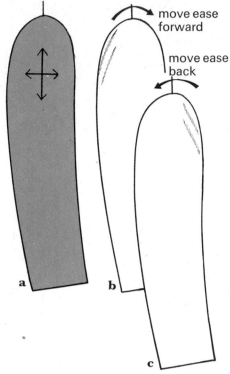

28 *Checking the sleeve:* **a** *correct;* **b** *creases towards back;* **c** *creases towards front*

27) and baste the sleeves into the arm-holes. Add shoulder pads if required.

The fitting stages

Check all the points made in the former fitting. Turn up the hem. If the coat has a tie or buckled belt, put on the belt before adjusting the hem as the length will be affected. Other belts are positioned after the hem has been turned up. The coat must not be cut in half by a belt, it should give a balanced, pleasing look. Check the length again with the belt in position. Check that the sleeve is not too tight or too loose. Turn up the sleeve hem.

Set in sleeve

Take a good look at each sleeve head. The grain should be square and there should be no creases (Fig. 28a).

If creases form towards the back, un-baste and move the ease slightly towards the front (Fig. 28b). If this is not enough then unbaste the complete sleeve and move it forwards. If there are creases towards the front then reverse the

process moving the ease to the back (Fig. 28c).

Raglan sleeve

Check that the sleeves are not too full at the shoulder. Any fullness should be pinned into the dart or seam which runs down the shoulder into the arm.

Terms and stitches

Ladder stitch: used for invisibly stitching a pocket to a garment.

Above. *An attractive three-quarter length cape, Butterick pattern 8416.*

Side stitch: used for flattening edges of lapels and collars. Make a tiny stitch at right angles to the line of stitching. The stitches should not appear on the right side of the garment.

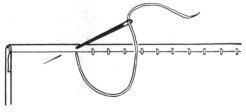

Step five

Plain tailored sleeve

Coat sleeves must be well fitted and have a crisp finish at the hem. With a two piece tailored sleeve there is usually ease at the elbow level and great care must be taken while basting and stitching to keep this in the correct position and so prevent the sleeve from twisting.

Stitching the sleeve

After fitting the sleeves unpick the armhole basting. Thread mark the length (Fig. 1). Mark any seam alterations. On a one piece sleeve unbaste the sleeve seam. On a two piece sleeve unbaste the back sleeve seam only (Fig. 2), stitch the front sleeve seam and press open. If the sleeve has ease in it stitch carefully and press as for an eased seam.

Finishing the hem edge

Cut a strip of interfacing in the crosswise grain of the fabric to the width of the sleeve and 5cm (2in) deep. Baste to the wrong side of the sleeve just above the hem line and catch stitch (Fig. 3). Turn up the hem and press. Catch stitch to the interfacing.

Gauntlet cuff

For a gauntlet cuff (Fig. 4) it is not necessary to interface the sleeve hem as it would be too bulky.

Cutting the pattern

Place the two pieces of sleeve pattern together with the lower part of the front seam lines coinciding, and the hem and back seam allowances turned back. Cut the cuff pattern extending it 0.6cm (¼in) each side at the hem edge and extending the top edge as style dictates. This cuff can be anything from 5cm to 10cm (2 to 4in) deep (Fig. 5).

Making the cuff

Using this pattern cut two pieces of coat fabric for each cuff adding 1.3cm (½in) seam allowance on the sides and top edge and 4cm (1½in) at the hem edge. Tailor's tack all round the pattern (Fig. 6).
Cut interfacing exactly to pattern, without seam allowance, and catch stitch to the under cuff section (Fig.7). Stitch the cuffs together along the top edge (Fig. 8a) then fold and stitch narrow ends together (Fig. 8b).

Place the right side of the faced under cuff section to the right side of the sleeve. The cuff stitching line should be 1.3cm (½in) above the sleeve hem line and the cuff seam corresponding to the back sleeve seam (Fig. 9). Stitch, trim seam allowance to 1.3cm (½in). Fold the top cuff over and baste along the top through both cuff layers only (Fig. 10). Baste at hem through all fabric layers. Turn the sleeve to the wrong side and catch stitch the lower edge of the cuff (Fig. 11), turning under the raw edge to neaten.

Strap cuff

A strap cuff (Fig. 12) usually lies from the front seam of a two piece sleeve to the back seam, across the top of the sleeve.

Cutting the pattern

Make a pattern for the strap, using the top sleeve pattern piece to give the correct angle (Fig. 13). These straps usually end 2.5cm (1in) from the back sleeve seam. Cut the cuff from the double fabric allowing 1.3cm (½in) all round for seams (Fig. 14). For each

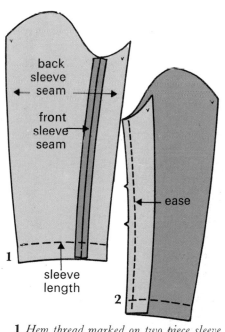

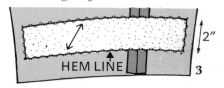

1 Hem thread marked on two piece sleeve
2 Stitching the front sleeve seam

3 Interfacing catch stitched in place to the sleeve hem line

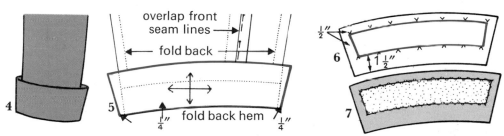

4 A gauntlet cuff 5 The pattern 6 Tailor's tacked details 7 The interfaced under cuff.

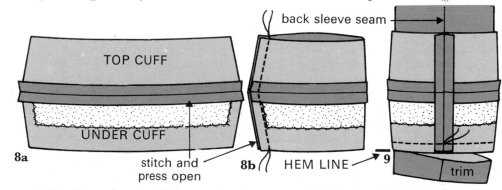

8 Stitching a gauntlet cuff. a top edge; b narrow ends 9 Under cuff stitched to sleeve

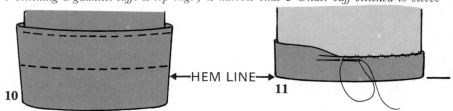

10 Basting the cuff in position 11 The finished gauntlet from the wrong side

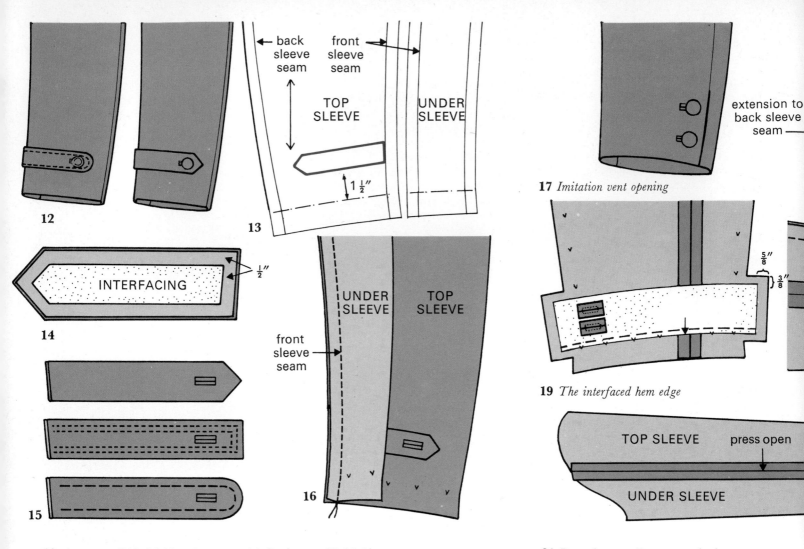

12 *A strap cuff* **13** *Making the pattern* **14** *Cutting out* **15** *Making up*
16 *Positioning the strap cuff on a sleeve*

17 *Imitation vent opening*

19 *The interfaced hem edge*

21 *Pressed seam allowance on back seam*

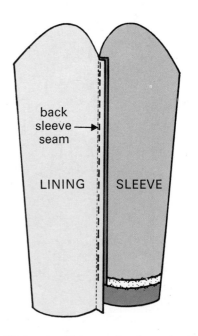

27 *Basting lining to the sleeve along the back sleeve seam*

strap cut one piece of interfacing to pattern without seam allowance.

Making the cuff
Make up the cuff as for the ¼ belt (Fig. 15). Baste to the front sleeve seam before the seam is made up (Fig. 16). Finish as for a plain sleeve.

Imitation vent opening on sleeve
Decide whether you would like this sleeve finish before you cut out the coat as additions have to made to the back sleeve seam (Fig. 17).

The pattern
Cut an extension to each side of the back sleeve seam (Fig. 18). The extension should be 3cm (1¼in) wide by the depth of the vent plus (⅜in) top and bottom for seam allowance.

Making up
Stitch the front sleeve seam and baste the interfacing to hem (Fig. 19). Make button holes on upper sleeve if required. Baste and stitch the back sleeve seam (Fig. 20). Snip the seam allowance on the under sleeve to allow the vent to lie on the top of the sleeve. Then press the sleeve seam open above and below the vent (Fig. 21). Press the lower vent seam up and then press the hem up to the vent opening and catch-stitch to interfacing (Fig. 22).

Two piece sleeve with vent opening
Cut a strip of interfacing on the cross, wide enough to reach the top of the opening by the sleeve width, without the seam allowance (Fig. 23). Make piped buttonholes to match the coat if required.
The next step is to mitre the corners (Fig. 24). Cut away the corners 0.3cm (⅛in) from the interfacing. Fold up the 0.3cm (⅛in) and press. Turn hem up and sides in, snipping at top of opening. Catch stitch to canvas and draw stitch mitred ends together. Stitch the back sleeve seam. Snip 0.6cm (¼in) above vent then press seam

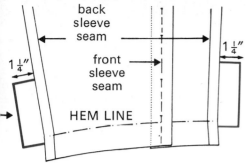

18 *Cutting extension on back sleeve seam*

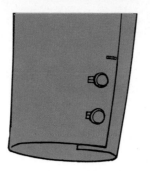

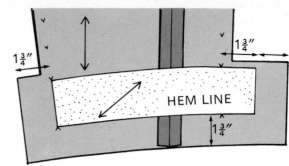

23 *Vent opening with interfacing at hem edge*

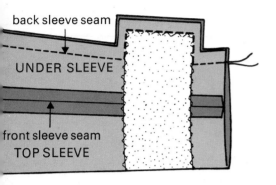

20 *Stitching the back sleeve seam*

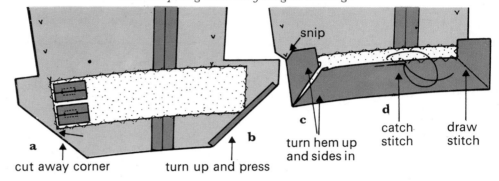

24 *Mitring the corners of a vent opening :* **a** *trimming the corners ;* **b** *the corners folded and pressed ;* **c** *turning in the seam allowance ;* **d** *drawing the mitred ends together*

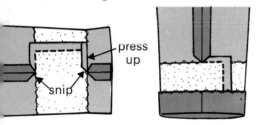

22 *The hem catch stitched in place*

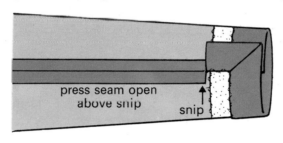

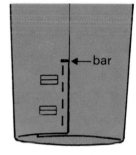

25 *Back sleeve seam stitched and pressed* **26** *Vent opening complete with bar tack*

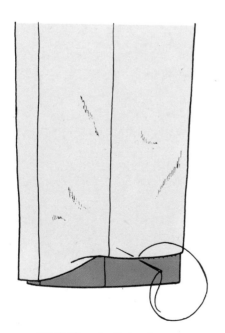

28 *Felling the lining hem*

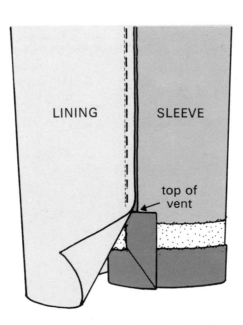

29 *Basting lining in sleeve with vent opening*

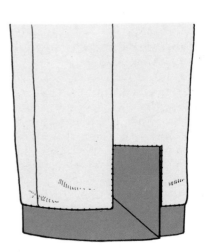

30 *The lining hem of sleeve with a vent*

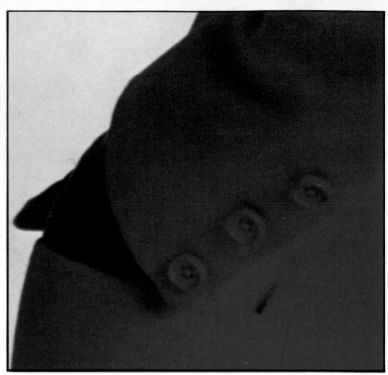

Sleeve detail of a plain cuff

Sleeve detail of a vent opening

open above snip and together below snip (Fig. 25). Baste vent in closed position and make a bar tack at the top of the opening (Fig. 26).

Lining a sleeve
The sleeve lining is sewn in place before the sleeve is stitched to the coat. It is much easier to do this now without the whole weight of the coat to contend with.

Plain sleeve lining
The method used here is also applied to a sleeve with an imitation vent, cuff or strap finish. Make up the sleeve lining and press the seams open.
With wrong sides out, place the sleeve and lining side by side with back sleeve seams corresponding (Fig. 27). Baste together along the sleeve line. Turn the lining right side out over the sleeve. Turn in the hem allowance of the lining and fell to the sleeve (Fig. 28).

Sleeve with a vent
Make up the sleeve lining, leaving the appropriate seam open below the vent. With wrong sides out, place the sleeve and lining side by side, with the back sleeve seams corresponding. Baste seams together above the vent. (Fig. 29). Turn the lining right side out over the sleeve. Turn the lining raw edges under as shown and baste. Fell lining to the sleeve (Fig. 30).

Terms and stitches
Bar tack: used to strengthen the top of a pleat or opening, and can be decorative as well as functional.
Using matching thread make a bar of 4 stitches. Oversew tightly along the length of the stitches.

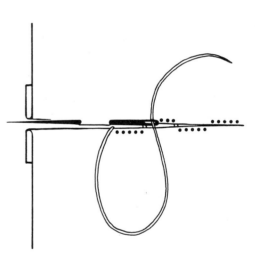

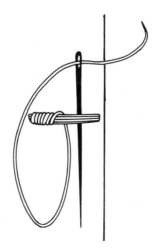

Draw stitch: used to close two folds of material together. Slip the needle through the top fold for 0.6cm (¼in). Then, directly under the end of the first stitch, slip the needle through the lower fold for 0.6cm (¼in).

Felling: this is a firm form of hemming with a stitch at right angles to the hem or fold.

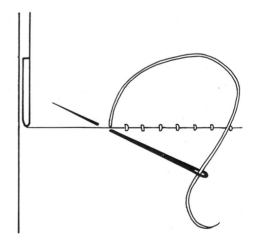

Step six

Making a step collar

The collar of a coat should be smooth and well fitting, so great care must be taken not to distort it when stitching and pressing. The collar is sewn to the coat by hand to ensure a perfect fit.

The under collar

Stitch the centre back seam. Trim the seam allowance to 0.6cm ($\frac{1}{4}$in) and press open (Fig. 1). Working on the under collar canvas, trim the centre back seam allowance to 0.6cm ($\frac{1}{4}$in), overlap on sewing line and stitch. Lay the canvas to the wrong side of the under collar with centre backs matching. Pin along the crease line, then run a taut thread along the crease line in matching thread (Fig. 2).

The crease line on the collar divides the stand from the fall (Fig. 3). Fold the undercollar on the crease line with the canvas side up, and pad stitch the fall, keeping within the stitching lines all round (Fig. 4). Work with the crease line away from you and work up and down in staggered lines. Similarly, pad stitch the stand, again working with the crease line away from you (Fig. 5).

Pressing the collar pieces

To fit the coat correctly the under and top collar pieces need to be pressed and moulded before being stitched together. Lay the under collar, right side down, on an ironing board (Fig. 6). Using a damp cloth press the fall, gently pulling the outer edge of the collar slightly, just above the shoulder position. Always pull towards the centre back as this must not be stretched. The edge should not be stretched more than 1.3cm ($\frac{1}{2}$in). Repeat for the stand (Fig. 7).

Turn under collar right side up and lay it flat on an ironing board with the stand folded over on the crease line. Using a damp cloth press firmly without stretching (Fig. 8). While the under collar is still damp, curve it around a pudding basin, with the stand turned in, to dry into a curve (Fig. 9). Prepare the top collar similarly, but turning the stand under.

Stitching the collar

Working on the under collar, trim the canvas to just inside the stitching line (Fig. 10). Check that the under collar fits neatly into the neck line with the ends matching (Fig. 11). Place the top and under collar pieces together, with right sides facing. Baste along crease

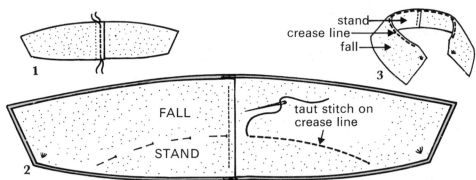

1 *Joining under collar canvas along the centre back* **2** *Sewing canvas to under collar along crease line* **3** *The stand and fall on a collar*

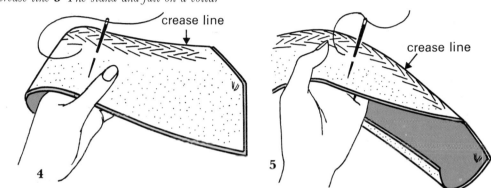

Pad stitching the canvas to the under collar: **4** *On the fall* **5** *On the stand*

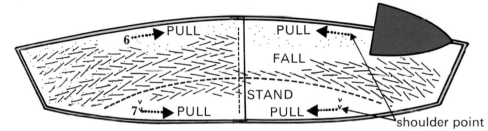

6 *Pressing and pulling fall of under collar* **7** *Pressing and pulling stand of under collar*

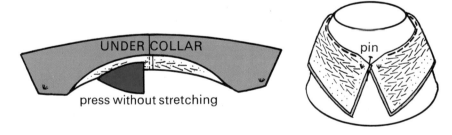

8 *Pressing the under collar*   **9** *Curving under collar round pudding basin*

line and along outside and step edges (Fig. 12).

Stitch and layer seams and snip corners (Fig. 13). Turn the collar to the right side and work the corners or curves into a good shape. Working on the under side, baste along the stitched edges keeping the seam rolled to the underside. Side stitch the seam edges to keep them in place (Fig. 14).

Turn under the seam allowance on the neck edge of the under collar and

baste (Fig. 15). Snip into the neck edge seam allowance of the top collar at the shoulder points. Turn under the seam allowance from the front edges to the shoulder point and baste. Press the collar very carefully.

Attaching the collar to the coat

Lay the coat, right side up, over your knees with the neck line towards you. Lay the under collar to the neck edge of the coat, right side up, with the

Coat with step collar

Coat with fitted collar

Coat with mandarin collar

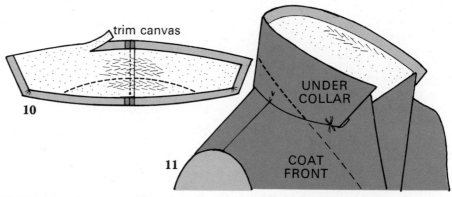

10 *Trimming the canvas on the under collar* **11** *Checking the fit of the under collar*

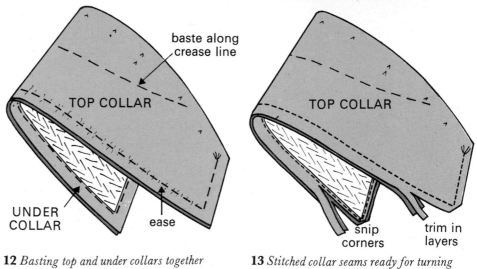

12 *Basting top and under collars together*   **13** *Stitched collar seams ready for turning*

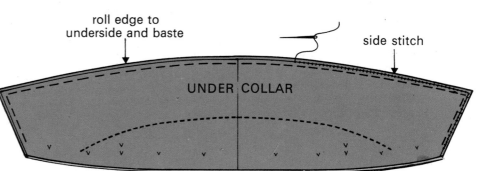

14 *The stitched edges of the turned collar basted and side stitched in place*

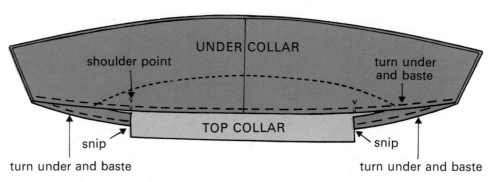

15 *Turning under and basting the neck edges of the collar ready for attaching to coat*

folded edge of the under collar meeting the sewing line of the coat neck edge. Carefully match the centre backs, shoulder points and crease line. Pin along the neck edge distributing the ease evenly (Fig. 16). Fell the collar to the coat, starting at the centre back and working to each end (Fig. 17). Finish the ends off securely.

Still with the coat on your knees, turn the coat over to the wrong side. Pad stitch the end of the bridle firmly to the crease of the collar (Fig. 18a). Turn in the seam allowance of the facings along the neck edge in a smooth line and baste to coat. (Fig. 18b).

Put the folded edges of the top collar to the folds of the facing. Using a draw stitch, draw the folds together making the stitches invisible (Fig. 19). The raw edge at the back of the top collar is herringboned down (Fig. 20). This is eventually covered by the lining. Press the neck seam carefully over a ham.

Making a fitted collar

A fitted collar is worked exactly as for the step collar. The crease line on a fitted collar runs from centre front (Fig. 21).

Making a mandarin collar

Like the step collar, the mandarin collar is also attached to the coat by hand. Cut a strip of wool and hair canvas to the shape of the collar without seam allowance. Catch stitch to the inside collar pieces (Fig. 22). Place the collar pieces together, with right sides facing. Baste and stitch, starting and ending at the neck seam line. Layer the seams and snip corners. Fold the neck seam allowances to the wrong side and baste. Turn the collar to the right side, working corners into a good shape. Baste and press (Fig. 23 and 24).

Sew the mandarin collar to the coat as for the step collar, in the position indicated on the pattern, remembering that the under collar is now facing inwards (Fig. 25).

Setting in the sleeves

Pinning

Make sure that the sleeves are put into their correct armholes. This might sound a silly thing to say but a mistake can easily be made.

Turn the coat wrong side out. Put the sleeve into the armhole with the right side of the sleeve facing the right side of the coat.

Working from inside the sleeve, pin all matching points (Fig. 26), incorporating any alterations made during the second fitting.

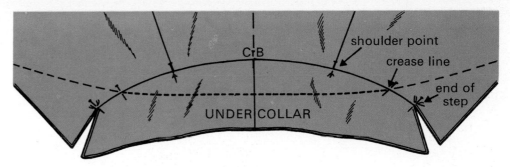

16 *Pinning the under collar to the coat neck edge*

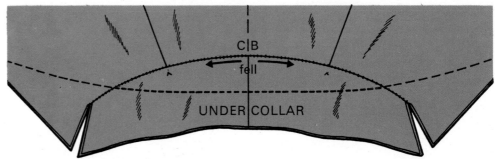

17 *Felling the under collar to the coat neck edge*

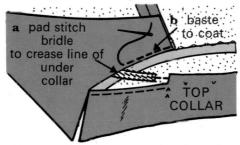

18a *Stitching the bridle extension;* **b** *turning in neck edge of front coat facing*

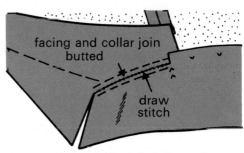

19 *Drawing the folds of the facing and top collar together invisibly*

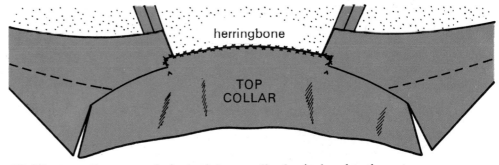

20 *The seam allowance at the back of the top collar herringboned to the coat*

Smooth fitted sleeve head

Hold the coat with the armhole seam rolled back over the fingers. Pin away the ease between the pins already in place (Fig. 27). Baste with small stitches.

Gathered sleeve head

Some fashion coats are being designed with a slight gather at the sleeve head (Fig. 28). Run a gathering thread as shown in the pattern instructions. Pin in the sleeve, then pull this thread until the sleeve head fits the armhole. Make sure that the gathers are even, then pin and baste with small stitches (Fig. 29).

The third fitting

Position shoulder pads if needed and put on the coat to have a final look

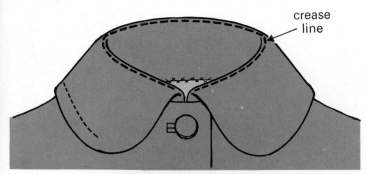

21 *The crease line on a fitted collar*

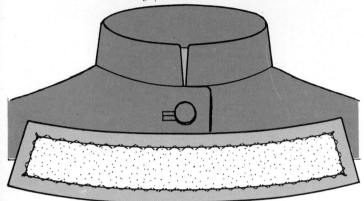

22 *The canvas on the inside collar piece of a mandarin collar*

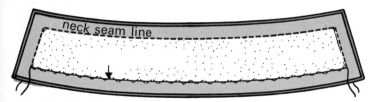

23 *Stitching the mandarin collar*

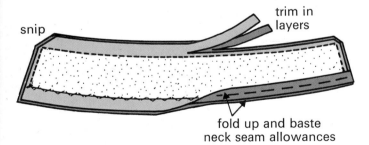

24 *The mandarin collar prepared for turning*

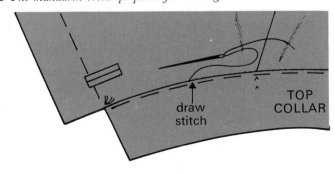

25 *Stitching the mandarin collar to the coat*

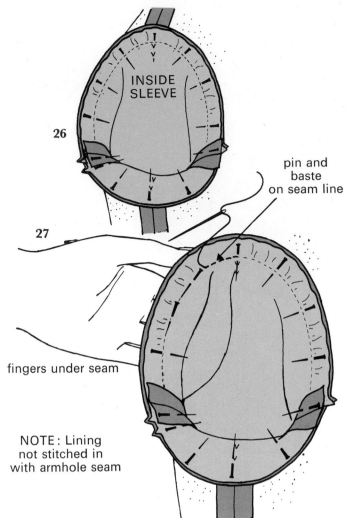

NOTE: Lining not stitched in with armhole seam

26 *Aligning and pinning matching points on sleeve and armhole*
27 *Pinning away the ease on the sleeve head*

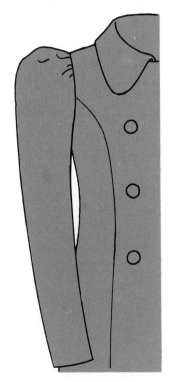

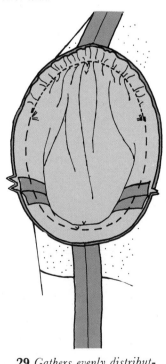

28 *Gathered sleeve head*

29 *Gathers evenly distributed and basted on gathered sleeve head*

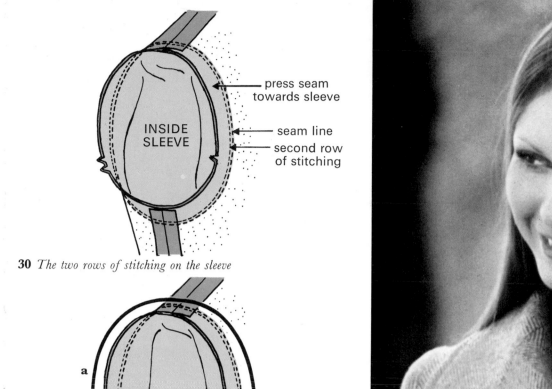

30 *The two rows of stitching on the sleeve*

31 *Cutting the sleeve padding:* **a** *measuring the length of the padding;* **b** *shaping the padding*

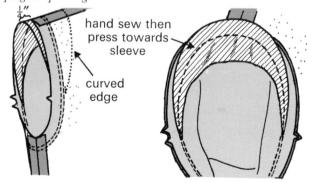

32 *Positioning the padding* **33** *Hand sewing the padding in place*

Detail of padded, smooth headed set in sleeve

at the sleeves. Ask a friend to help you as the hang of the sleeves alters with the movement and you need to be perfectly still to get the correct set.

Also check that there is enough ease across the back when you make natural movements, such as sitting in a driving position or pushing a pram. It is a good idea to give the length a final check too.

Stitching in the sleeves

The sleeves can be machine stitched or hand sewn in place with back stitch.

Always work from inside the sleeve as the fullness can be controlled this way. Make a second row of stitching in the seam allowance 0.3cm ($\frac{1}{8}$in) outside the first row (Fig. 30). Without trimming the seam press it towards the sleeve, shrinking the sleeve seam carefully at the top.

Sleeve head padding

Padding the sleeve head gives a slightly rounded look to a smooth head and will support the shape of a gathered one.

Measure the length over the shoulder from the back balance mark to the front balance mark (Fig. 31a). Cut two pieces of tailor's wadding to that length and shape (Fig. 31b).

Place the curved side to the sleeve so that the padding extends 0.6cm ($\frac{1}{4}$in) at the sleeve head (Fig. 32). Using matching thread, hand sew the pad firmly in place on the second line of stitches, working through all thicknesses of the fabric (Fig. 33).

Step seven

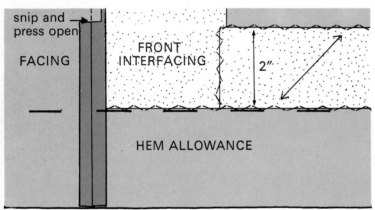

1 *Thread marking the hem line*

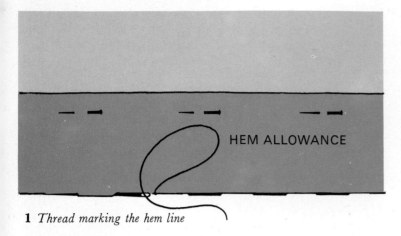

2 *The canvas sewn along a straight hem edge*

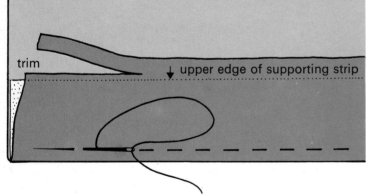

3 *Basting the hem edge ¼ inch above the fold*

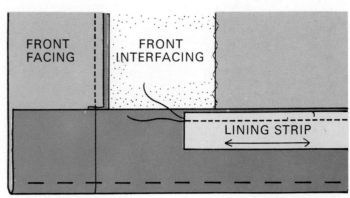

4 *Positioning the lining strip along the hem allowance*

5 *Turning in the lining strip*

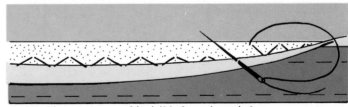

6 *Sewing the hem with invisible hemming stitch*

7 *Working two rows of invisible hemming stitch*

Sewing the hem

Straight hem

These instructions are for a coat which has a perfectly straight hem edge or is only very slightly curved. Thread mark the fold of the hem then remove the pins (Fig. 1). To give the hem a good crisp finish, support the hem edge with strips of duck or canvas. Cut the strips 5cm (2in) wide on the cross of the fabric and to the length of the coat hem edge, joining if necessary to make up the required length. Sew to the hem edge with catch stitch (Fig. 2).

Turn up the hem and baste flat 0.6cm (¼in) above the fold (Fig. 3). Press well, making sure that the iron does not impress the hem edge into the fabric. Measure the hem depth to just above the supporting strips and trim.

To bind the seam allowance on the hem, cut 2.5cm (1in) wide strips of coat lining fabric on the straight of the grain. The selvedge is useful for this. Position the lining strip on the hem edge, but, to avoid bulk, do not continue the binding along the part of the hem which will be under the front facings (Fig. 4). Stitch, taking 0.6cm (¼in) seam allowance. Fold the binding to the wrong side and baste (Fig. 5). Press, making sure the hem lies away from the coat otherwise impressions will be left on the coat fabric.

Baste the hem in place matching seams. Then, with the folded hem edge towards you lift the hem slightly and sew neatly to the canvas with invisible hemming

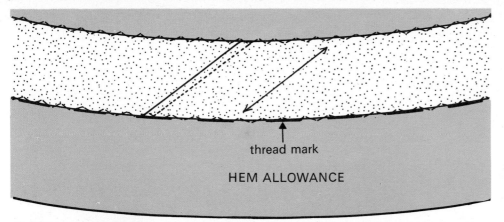

8 *The canvas sewn along a curved hem edge*

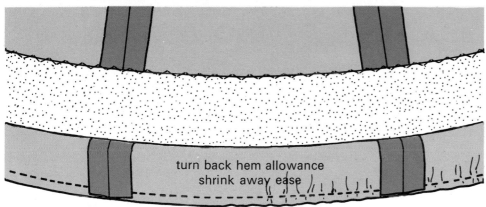

9 *Pulling in the fullness of a curved hem*

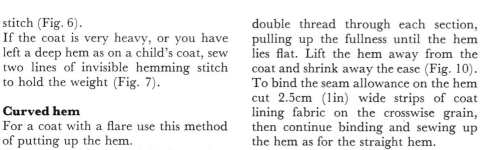

10 *Shrinking the eased hem*

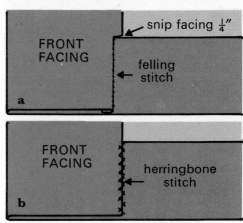

11 *Finishing the hem at the facing:* **a** *on a thin fabric:* **b** *on a thick fabric*

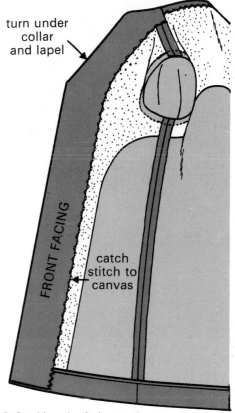

12 *Catching the facing to the canvas*

stitch (Fig. 6).

If the coat is very heavy, or you have left a deep hem as on a child's coat, sew two lines of invisible hemming stitch to hold the weight (Fig. 7).

Curved hem

For a coat with a flare use this method of putting up the hem.

First work as for a straight hem edge, gently easing the canvas into position around the curve of the coat hem (Fig. 8).

Turn the hem up and baste flat 0.6cm (¼in) above the fold, then trim the hem edge to just above the supporting strips as for the straight hem. Matching centre backs and fronts and seam lines, pin the hem (Fig. 9). Then run a

double thread through each section, pulling up the fullness until the hem lies flat. Lift the hem away from the coat and shrink away the ease (Fig. 10). To bind the seam allowance on the hem cut 2.5cm (1in) wide strips of coat lining fabric on the crosswise grain, then continue binding and sewing up the hem as for the straight hem.

Finishing the facing

Place the coat down on a flat surface and turn the facing to the inside. There are two ways of finishing off the hem edge:

On thin fabrics first snip into the facing seam allowance at the top of the hem. Then turn the facing under 0.6cm (¼in) at the hem edge and fell firmly

in place to the hem seam allowance (Fig. 11a). On thick fabrics do not turn under the raw edge to neaten, but simply herringbone the raw edge in position (Fig. 11b).

To finish off the facing, lay the coat down flat, facing side up and lapel turned under. Catch stitch the facing to the canvas (Fig. 12).

Finishing piped buttonholes

With the facing now in its final position it is time to finish the back of the piped buttonholes.

Working from the right side, push a pin through to the wrong side at each end of the buttonhole to find the exact position of the slit on the facing. Make a slit through the facing between the

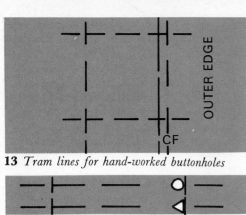

13 *Tram lines for hand-worked buttonholes*

14 *The outer edge of the hand-worked buttonhole:* **a** *circle;* **b** *a triangle*

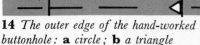

15 *The cut buttonhole*

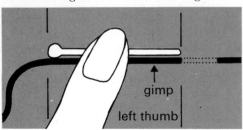

16 *Oversewing the buttonhole with single thread*

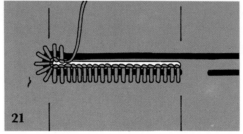

17 *Gimp laid along the buttonhole*

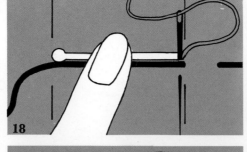

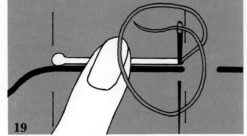

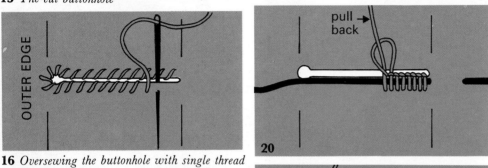

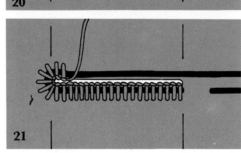

18 to 21 *Working the buttonhole*

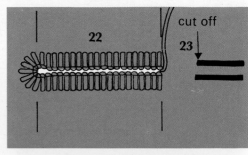

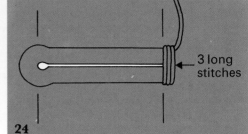

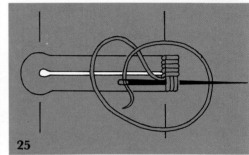

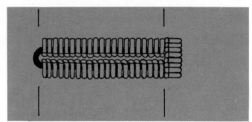

22 to 25 *Working the buttonhole continued*

26 *A sham buttonhole*

pins and mitre the corners just beyond the pins. Fold under the raw edges and fell securely in place.
Finally, press on the wrong side.

Hand-worked buttonholes
Tailored, hand-worked buttonholes are beautiful when sewn evenly, so practice on a double piece of the fabric with interfacing in between before starting on the garment itself. The thread to use is silk buttonhole twist and you will also need buttonhole gimp. An alternative to buttonhole gimp is two threads of buttonhole twist waxed together to prevent them untwisting.
Prepare buttonhole tram lines (Fig. 13). Using a stilletto make a round hole at the outer edge of the buttonhole (Fig. 14a), or cut out a triangle (Fig. 14b). Continuing from the hole, cut the length of the buttonhole. Cut very carefully as a jagged line shows up

on the finished buttonhole (Fig. 15). Using a single strand of matching thread, oversew round the buttonhole through all thicknesses (Fig. 16).
Lay the gimp to the buttonholes. The gimp is held in place with the thumb when working the buttonhole (Fig. 17). Thread the needle with a long length of buttonhole twist so you will have enough to finish the buttonhole without joining.
Starting at the point shown and working with the right side of the coat facing you, insert the needle through the back of the buttonhole making sure that all layers of the fabric are caught (Fig 18). Take the thread forward under the needle (Fig. 19). Pull the needle through and tighten the loop with the thread pulled back, so that the knot lies on the cut edge of the buttonhole (Fig. 20).
At the circle or triangle fan the

stitches out wider at the outer edge of the curve (Fig. 21).
Complete the other side of the buttonhole but do not cut the thread off yet (Fig. 22). Pull the gimp tight, thread between the layers of fabric and cut off (Fig. 23).
To make the bar tack at the end of the buttonhole work three long stitches as shown for the bar. Work buttonhole stitch over the bar and through the fabric, bringing the knots to the top (Fig. 24 and 25).

Sham buttonholes
Sham buttonholes are sometimes made for vents.
Without cutting a slit, work buttonhole stitch along the buttonhole line (Fig. 26). Make a bar tack at the end but omit the circle at the front end, as the button covers the lack of circle.

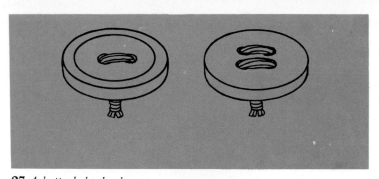

27 *A buttonhole shank*

28 *Starting the shank and positioning the button*

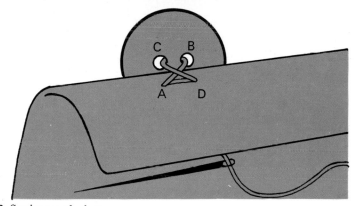

29 *Sewing on the button*

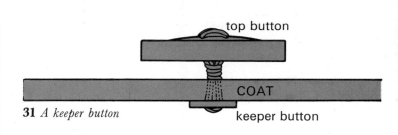

30 *Making the shank*

31 *A keeper button*

32a, b *Sewing on a keeper button.*

The final press

Lay the coat right side up on a board. Using a wool pressing cloth under a slightly damp cotton cloth, gently press all over the coat, moving each section of the coat so that it lies flat as you press it.

This process needs to be done with hardly any pressure on the iron to avoid making impressions on the coat. Hang the coat to dry before lining.

Sewing on the buttons

Before the coat is lined the buttons should be sewn on.

Making a shank

A flat button should be sewn on with a shank so that the button does not distort the buttonhole by being too close to the fabric (Fig. 27).

Using a strong buttonhole thread, take a back stitch through the fabric at the button position. Do not use a knot. Fold the coat back and hold the button in position (Fig. 28 and 29).

Take the thread from 'a' through holes 'b' and then 'c', then back into fabric at 'd'. Repeat three or four times, and again if the button has four holes. This gives crossed threads which make a strong foundation for the shank.

With the thread coming out from 'c' wind it tightly round the shank (Fig. 30). Take the thread to the back and fasten off securely to finish.

Keeper button

For added strength a little keeper button can be sewn onto the back of the coat at the same time as the top button is being sewn on (Fig. 31).

The keeper button should be a tiny button with the same number of holes as the top button.

Lay the top button over two match-sticks and sew on the button, at the same time sewing through the matching holes on the keeper button (Fig. 32). Leave the thread quite loose. Remove the matchsticks and make a shank.

Terms and stitches
Invisible hemming stitch

Step eight

pleat

turn under collar and lapels

tuck in sleeves

fasten buttons

1 *The stitched lining*

← **turn under ⅛″ and stitch**

2 *Neatening the lining seam allowances*

3 *Positioning coat on a tailor's dummy*

4a

4a, b *Pinning lining to coat (front and back)*

Lining a coat

The outside of the coat is now finished, and all that remains is for the coat to be lined. A lining covers the seams and prolongs the life of a coat and also makes it easier to wear.

Cutting and stitching the lining

Cut the lining according to the pattern instructions, bearing in mind any alterations you have made to the coat.

Pin baste and stitch any darts or pleats (Fig. 1). Then pin, baste and stitch all seams except for the shoulder and armhole seams. Neaten the seam allowances by turning under the edges for 0.3cm (⅛in) and stitching (Fig. 2). Iron the lining well, but be sure to test the iron temperature first.

Putting in the lining

If you have a tailor's dummy, put the coat on it, wrong side out, tucking the sleeves flat to the sides. Fasten the coat buttons and adjust the coat to hang correctly (Fig. 3).

If you do not have a dummy, lay the coat right side down on a table.

As you work on a section lay it as flat as possible.

Pin the lining to the coat, wrong sides together (Fig. 4a and b). Start at the centre back of the neck and do not

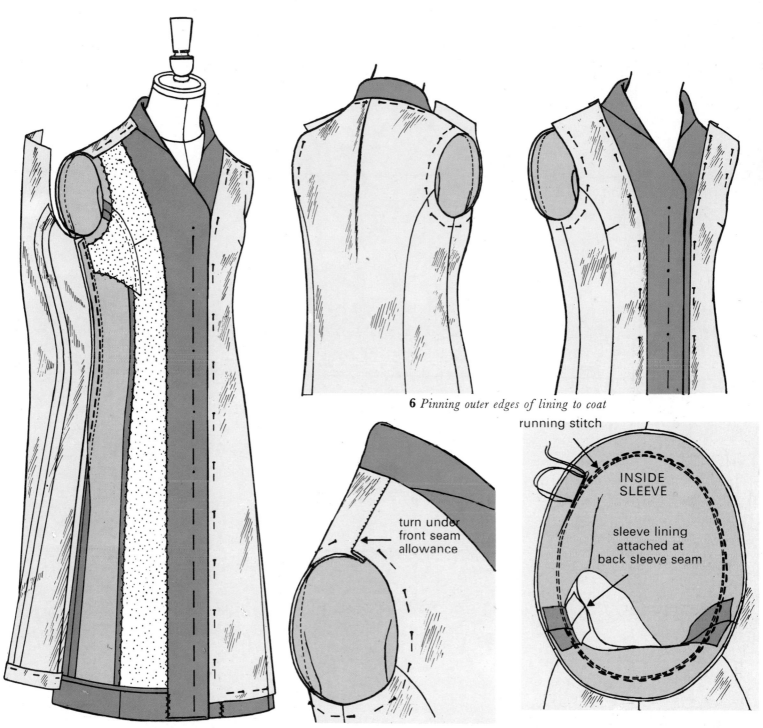

5 *Basting coat side seam allowance to lining*

6 *Pinning outer edges of lining to coat*

running stitch

INSIDE SLEEVE

sleeve lining attached at back sleeve seam

7 *Felling the lining shoulder seams*

turn under front seam allowance

8 *Sewing the lining armhole seam allowances to the coat*

turn under the raw seam allowances at the edges of the lining.

Pin in this order:

Round back neck, after pleating centre back as shown in pattern instructions.

Down any style seams at the back

The side seams.

The front style seams or darts.

Down the front.

Round the armholes. If the armholes have been stretched during making do

not cut the lining to match. Instead, ease the coat onto the lining to avoid distorting it.

Along the shoulder seams, overlapping the seams over any shoulder pads if used.

Down the centre back pleat if there is one.

Turn up the lining hem 2.5cm (1in) above the coat hem and pin.

Slip on the coat to see if the lining is

pulling at any point. Once again it is best if a friend can help you.

Lift the lining, baste the side seam allowances of coat and lining together from underarm to hip level, unpinning where necessary (Fig. 5).

Turn under the seam allowances along the neck and front edges of the lining and repin to facing (Fig. 6). Turn up the hem and fell firmly.

On each shoulder turn under the front

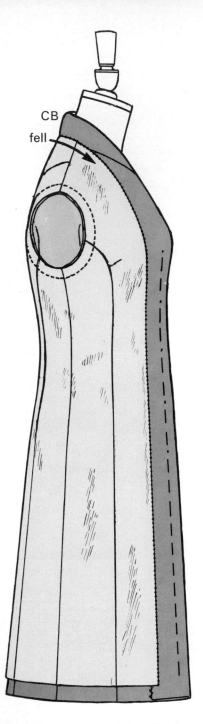

9 *Felling the outer edges of lining to coat*

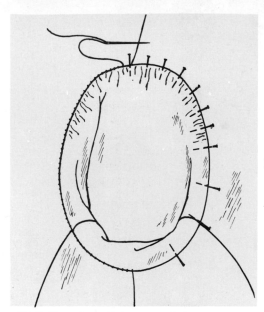

10 *Felling sleeve lining to armhole seam*

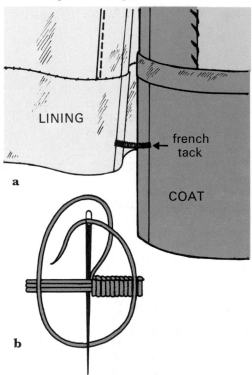

a

b

11a, b *Making a french tack*

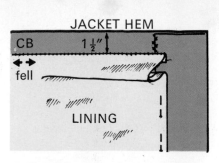

12 *Felling lining hem edge on a jacket*

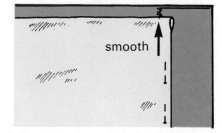

13 *Smoothing down the jacket lining*

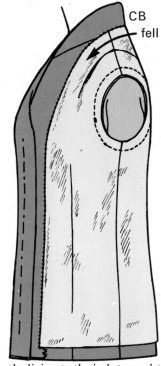

14 *Felling the lining to the jacket round the outer edges*

shoulder seam allowances on the lining and position over the back seam allowance and fell (Fig. 7).

Working from inside the sleeves, sew the lining to the coat just outside the sleeve stitching line (Fig. 8). Use a double thread and running stitch. Working from the centre back of the neck, fell the lining to the coat round the outer edges to the hem line (Fig. 9). It is now time to sew the lining armhole seams. Bring the sleeve lining up and turn in the seam allowance. Pin over the coat lining taking the ease into small gathers (Fig. 10). Fell firmly to the coat lining. Make french tacks at the hem

ends of the side seams to hold the lining to the hem.

French tack

To make a french tack first sew (3in to 4in) long stitches anchored to coat lining (Fig. 11a). Then, with the same thread, work buttonhole stitch over the entire lenth of the long stitches (Fig. 11b).

Lining a jacket

A jacket lining is attached in the same way as a coat lining except at the hem edge which is not left loose and attached with a french tack as on a coat. Pin the lining hem to the same length as the

jacket. Continue as for coat lining but lift the hem edge of the lining up 4cm (1½in) above the jacket edge. Fell to the jacket hem allowance along the entire length (Fig. 12). Smooth the front lining down into a fold at the hem edge (Fig. 13).

Starting at the centre back of the neck, fell the lining to the coat round the outer edges down to the fold at the hem (Fig. 14). The extra length in the lining provided by the fold at the hem allows for movement when wearing the jacket.

Finally sew the lining armhole seam as for a coat.